An Introduction to River Fishing

AN INTRODUCTION TO
RIVER FISHING

DAVID BATTEN

The Crowood Press

First published in 1990 by
The Crowood Press Ltd
Ramsbury, Marlborough
Wiltshire SN8 2HR

Paperback edition 1993

British Library Cataloguing-in-Publication Data

A catalogue record for this book is available from the British Library

ISBN 1 85223 760 0

Photographs by David Batten and John Wilson
Line-drawings by David Batten

Typeset by PCS Typesetting, Frome, Somerset
Printed and bound in Great Britain by
BPCC Hazell Books Ltd
Member of BPCC Ltd

Contents

Acknowledgements

Despite any book being the author's own work, much of what he writes is bound to have been influenced by contact with others up to the point of putting pen to paper. It will not have been apparent, at the particular moment in time, that a contribution was made, but later, when there is time to reflect, we all recognise that we were influenced or guided by friends and contacts. With this in mind, it is only right that I express my thanks to all those who may have influenced me in angling and in the writing of this series of books.

Particular mention must be made of those who have directly helped with material and psychological support during the months spent researching, writing and illustrating – times when it seemed impossible that everything would come to fruition. Greatest thanks must go to my wife, Kathy, who has had the task of preparing the manuscripts and indexes, turning out at all hours of the night to help get photographs and generally putting up with an angler who has not been able to go fishing as and when he wished!

For their photographic contributions, my thanks go to Colin Brett, Chris Turnbull and John Wilson. Some special mention is due to John who, in the midst of his own pressures of filming and writing, gave up precious time to take photographs for the cover. Thanks also to Mike Wood for his assistance in getting photographic material and references for the illustrations, and for his pleasant company on many successful and not so successful sessions!

Introduction

Every season many people take up angling for the first time or return to it after a lay-off. Either way, many of those anglers will get started on some form of coarse fishing on one of their local still waters. That first tingle of interest may come from knowing somebody who catches a particular big fish or from reading about the capture of a particular fish in the local press. Many newcomers today get started by taking up carp fishing. Most of the tackle and reading matter, not to mention baits, are centred around this branch of the sport.

Depending on success or failure, many of those who start on carp will begin to look for some new direction and inspiration. The individual will undoubtedly start to think about all the other species there are to fish for.

There will be few anglers who have not thought about taking a day's fishing on rivers like the Hampshire Avon or the Thames, or perhaps one of their local rivers.

Perhaps that is why you were drawn to this book – you were thinking it might be nice to come to terms with fishing running water. Within the following pages you will find much of the inspiration you will require. The only other thing you will need is the opportunity to get on to one of our many rivers.

For those of you who already fish on running waters, there is the interest in reading another angler's view. Whether you fall into the first or second category, you will undoubtedly gain a great deal from the information in the text and many illustrations that follow. I hope you enjoy it!

1 Fisheries

A river fishery is a bit of an enigma because unless there is some means of holding fish within a particular stretch, they may move into a different area, rendering it almost fishless. Most river systems have a number of weirs or water-mills along their length and, within reason, it is these that constitute barriers to movement, thereby creating a fishery, to some degree. This is fine if the fishery extends the full distance from barrier to barrier, but what happens if a small angling club has a fishery with bank access of half a mile on a stretch of a mile or more between mills, locks etc.? In this situation it is possible that at any one time a high percentage of the fish inhabiting or stocked into the stretch, could be in the other section of the river. The fishery, as such, would be empty. Even where the whole stretch is available to be classified as a fishery, there is a possibility that all, or nearly all, the fry and a high percentage of mature fish could be lost from the stretch in times of high water and flood, if the mills or locks are opened up to run off excess water. This is a cause of failure on some rivers every winter when sluices are opened to keep the water level low to reduce the risk of flooding.

Whilst these situations cause fisheries to be poor in their own rights, life is made worse by the fact that clubs and fishery owners feel it would be wasting money and effort to stock or restock a stretch of river that cannot be controlled as a lake fishery can. Other factors in the decline of a river fishery can be pollution from farm waste or chemical spillage – either accidental or regardless of risk and the introduction of trout to any part of the section of river. Many landowners and trout fishery managers frown on coarse fish and actively pursue a policy of removing them from their stretch of the river.

FISHERY MANAGEMENT

There is no certain cure for this problem as many clubs will testify. The only answer is to fish for what fish are left. In many situations the remaining fish will be the larger specimens of each species. This has its benefits for those of us who seek them specifically, but that attitude will never see our rivers returned to their fullest potential. General stock levels need to be maintained. Many river fisheries that survive, do so in spite of rather than because of fishery management. If a definite policy of management was applied, perhaps more enthusiasm could be generated to protect our rivers. One solution is being pursued by the new National River Authority – 'Off River Supplementation Units', known affectionately as ORSUs (see Fig 1). This involves digging small ponds beside the river and connecting them to the river with an outlet controlled by a sluice gate. Into these ponds are placed freshly hatched fry which are left to grow through to autumn, when they are released as small fry into the river to grow (hopefully) into mature stock fish.

Perhaps if clubs and fishery owners were to carry out their own exercise, along the same lines, then the stocks could be enhanced

Middle section of the River Wissey.

further. It is highly likely that the River Authority would supply the fry to be grown on free of charge.

You will probably have found the preceding paragraphs a little heavy-going and of little interest to you, as an angler, simply seeking to catch fish. The reality is, unless you appreciate the implications of extraction, dewatering and pollution you may never get what you want from fishing in running water.

Moving back to the brighter side of the current situation of free-wheeling indigenous fish stocks, it is undoubtedly true to say that some fish thrive on neglect. There are stretches on many rivers that have suffered pollution or some similar fate which have not been fished for many years and it is quite possible that these are the areas to check out as fish may have re-colonised. Many a specimen has been caught by the inquisitive angler who has ventured to try one of these quiet stretches of river.

On most river systems there are different zones, the character of each varying to some degree. It may be that the river gushes fast and clear over chalk, in its upper reaches, moves down to wider and deeper less pacey stretches and eventually into tidal stretches where it may become much wider, deeper and slow moving (*see* Fig 2). Each of these zones will contain varying species. The faster upper section may contain grayling, trout, etc; the middle zone, barbel, chub, dace and roach; the lower slow-moving stretches, bream, tench, carp and roach, etc.

Rivers like the Hampshire Avon, the Kennet, the Wye, the Severn and the Trent typify this zoning. Many more are of a similar nature and you can probably think of a river in your own area in which you can identify these characteristics. The middle and lower stretches of the river are the ones we are concerned with and it would be of benefit to you to locate more than one river system to fish and more than one section on each river. Conditions will vary from area to area throughout the year and by having a fishery to suit the various conditions it will allow you to have somewhere to fish most of the time.

which river will fish in specific conditions, for a particular species, ensuring you maximise the opportunity to catch.

You should choose a fishery that is close enough to allow you to fish it easily – one that you can capitalise on when it is in its optimum condition and one on which you can regularly observe both the effects of weather and fish locations etc. Far more fish will fall to the angler who has located his quarry and who fishes for them at the best moment.

WEIRS

Rivers with weirs and plenty of flow will provide oxygenated water where fish can feel comfortable in hot conditions and will also offer open water in times of severe cold (*see* Fig 3). Careful selection will allow you to choose

PERMISSION TO FISH

Having located your fishery, the subject of access is of paramount importance. If you need to join a club to gain access, do so. If that section of river is private and to all intents and purposes unfished, it may be possible to

Tewkesbury Weir on the River Severn.

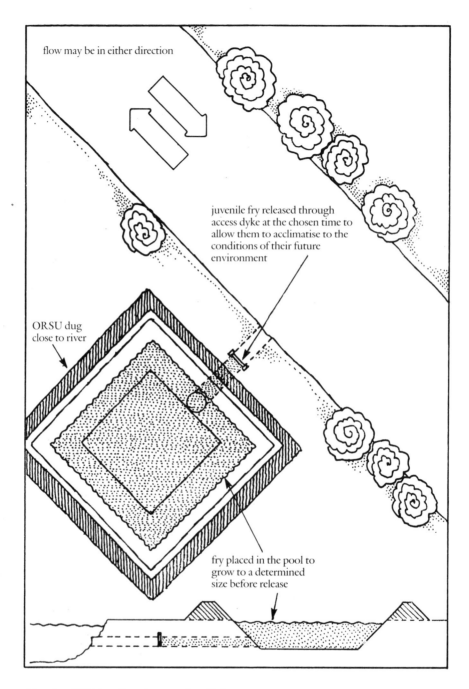

Fig 1   Off River Supplementation Unit
(ORSU).

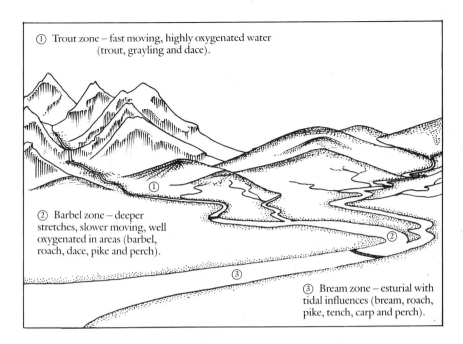

① Trout zone – fast moving, highly oxygenated water (trout, grayling and dace).

② Barbel zone – deeper stretches, slower moving, well oxygenated in areas (barbel, roach, dace, pike and perch).

③ Bream zone – esturial with tidal influences (bream, roach, pike, tench, carp and perch).

Fig 2   River zones.

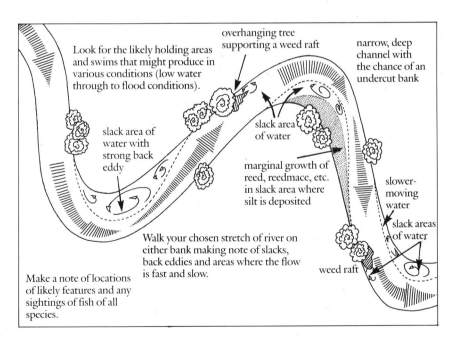

overhanging tree supporting a weed raft

narrow, deep channel with the chance of an undercut bank

Look for the likely holding areas and swims that might produce in various conditions (low water through to flood conditions).

slack area of water with strong back eddy

slack area of water

marginal growth of reed, reedmace, etc. in slack area where silt is deposited

slower-moving water

slack areas of water

Walk your chosen stretch of river on either bank making note of slacks, back eddies and areas where the flow is fast and slow.

weed raft

Make a note of locations of likely features and any sightings of fish of all species.

Fig 3   Features on the fishery.

Dobbs Weir on the River Lea.

A weedy run on the Upper Wissey.

The turbulent water of Tewkesbury Weir.

A River Wensum weed raft hotspot.

obtain access for a few days, or more, by locating the owners and politely asking permission. The important thing is to ask, and if no fee is required, you should still offer some gesture of thanks – a donation to a charity or a bottle of scotch. It may help you to get access to another stretch on another day.

Whilst on any river fishery, keep your eyes peeled for any signs of trouble for the fish, i.e. pollution, and notify both the owner and the River Authority immediately. Swift action may save a major disaster, in the form of a fish kill.

2 Tackle

Fishing in running waters for a variety of species places differing demands on the angler when it comes to tackle. It is possible to get by for many of the small to medium-size species with one rod and reel, however, to be able to cope with all the possible situations that an angler might be confronted with, you will need to become equipped with suitable tackle. The growth in pike and carp tackle has been accompanied by a steady growth in the specialist tackle available to the general angler. Indeed, many of the innovations aimed at the carp angler have opened new doors for others.

RODS

Without exception, every angler will have their own preference and opinion of what makes an ideal rod for a given situation. It may be that the angler has grown up with a rod gaining experience and reward over a long period of time. You probably have a rod which you always choose to use automatically. Many of the old favourite rods will be made of fibreglass and whilst these can still be effective, the advent of carbon fibre and, more lately, combined carbon/aramid fibre mixtures have given us very light positive-actioned rods which allow accurate casting and firm hook setting and feel whilst playing any hooked fish.

Casting

Fishing in running water, there is very little need for long-range casting (*see* Fig 4). The only time there will be more than fifteen to twenty yards between the angler and his bait is when long trotting. Then it might be possible to trot thirty or more yards to locate feeding fish but it is then far better to draw the fish up to within a more acceptable range.

Avon Action

Fishing at short range will place different demands on the angler and his tackle, depending on both the species sought and the water being fished. Roach and dace in medium-paced rivers will require a completely different rod to chub or barbel in either slow or fast-paced rivers. If ever there was a rod designed that went some way to covering these differing requirements, it must surely be the 'Avon', as originally conceived by Richard Walker in built cane. This was a ten-foot rod with a compound action that was at home both trotting and legering for numerous species. Since then there have been fibreglass and carbon copies of the design, most having a length of eleven or, more lately, twelve feet.

Right Choice

Today we have a whole host of manufacturers providing many varieties of rods aimed specifically at particular methods and species, most produced in top-quality materials. Listed in Tables 1 and 2 are some of the most popular makes and models and their relevant specifications. Before buying any rod it is well worth checking out as many of those on the market as

With many terminal tackles on small- to medium-sized rivers a simple side cast will get the bait and tackle into the swim. Position yourself so that you are facing exactly the spot you wish the bait to be. Begin the cast with a firm sweep and release the line as the tackle comes past the tip.

As you come to the end of the cast the rod tip will be pointing directly at the spot where you wish the bait to land. If you have used the correct force and weight you should get the bait in the correct spot.

Fig 4   Seated side casting.

A fine example of dace taken on the stick float.

Make and Model	Material	Length	Features
Drennan Light Feeder	Carbon	11ft	2 tips ¾ and 1½oz
Drennan Medium Feeder	Carbon	11½ft	2 tips 1½ and 2oz
Drennan Heavy Feeder	Carbon	12ft	2 tips 2 and 4oz
Diawa WK11TQTF Quiver Tip	Carbon/Kevlar	11ft	2 tips (light, medium
Diawa JCL10QT Quiver Tip	Carbon	10ft	3 tips and heavy)
Ryobi John Wilson Quiver Tip	Carbon	11ft	2 top sections (quiver and Avon float)

Table 1   Rods (leger).

Make and Model	Material	Length	Features
Diawa Harrier CWM13F	Carbon	13ft	
Diawa Vulcan VCM13F	Carbon	13ft	
Drennan Specialist	Carbon	12ft	Lines 3–7lb BS
Drennan Stickfloat	Carbon	13ft	Lines 1½–2½lb BS

Table 2   Rods (float).

possible, to ensure you obtain the very best value for the money you have. You will, I am afraid, only get what you pay for. If you spend £30 on a rod you will probably be disappointed; if you spend £90 on a top-quality rod in a carbon/aramid fibre you will have a durable, life-long tool which will, in the end, repay the high initial cost. Buy the best you can afford first time around.

Smooth Action

There are a few points to remember when choosing your rods. Check the fit of all the joints, whether spigot or over fit. These should be snug and should not 'knock' when the assembled rod is shaken and there should be a good space (at least a quarter of inch) between sections on spigotted rods to allow for wear to be taken up. With quiver tip rods there should be no 'flat spot' in the curve due to a poorly matched quiver tip being spliced into the blank and the quiver tip should bend almost fully before the blank begins to bend. A soggy blank that bends with the quiver tip is going to be useless, with no power in the lower section to apply pressure to set the hook or to apply pressure to a fish in a tight swim (see Fig. 5).

Specific Actions

With float rods, the type of action will be very important. A common misconception is that a so-called 'match' rod is ideal for all float fishing. How wrong that is and just how many people have been disappointed with a rod carrying such a description is beyond calculation. Thankfully, a few manufacturers have begun to recognise the need for rods designed to handle specific circumstances. We now have waggler rods, stickfloat rods and rods called specimen rods, built on the 'Avon' design

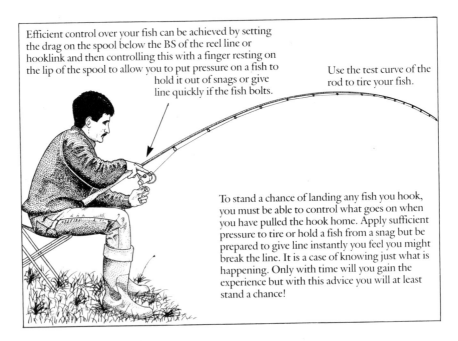

Efficient control over your fish can be achieved by setting the drag on the spool below the BS of the reel line or hooklink and then controlling this with a finger resting on the lip of the spool to allow you to put pressure on a fish to hold it out of snags or give line quickly if the fish bolts.

Use the test curve of the rod to tire your fish.

To stand a chance of landing any fish you hook, you must be able to control what goes on when you have pulled the hook home. Apply sufficient pressure to tire or hold a fish from a snag but be prepared to give line instantly you feel you might break the line. It is a case of knowing just what is happening. Only with time will you gain the experience but with this advice you will at least stand a chance!

Fig 5   Applying pressure to a hooked fish.

concept, for use on many species and using various methods.

Of course, the manufacturers of these rods would claim that we should all have at least one of each style of rod, but more to the point is the fact that we can now choose a rod to suit the circumstances we find ourselves in. This is a much more acceptable situation than having to fish three or four-pound line with a rod that was designed to handle lines of possibly three-quarters to one and half pound BS – fine for small roach and dace but not really the tool for big roach or chub.

REELS

As with rods, there has been a revolution in reel design. The most noticeable innovation is their reduction in weight as new materials are found. Most of these have come from aeros-pace technology and graphite composite materials are predominant in most makes of reel today. As well as being very lightweight, most are now made of non-corrosive components which prolongs their durability. These are fixed-spool design reels with bail arms fitted with silicon carbide, low-friction line rollers on 'never fail' over-centre return springs, that ensure the bail will always operate at an optimum level. There are skirted spools preventing tangles around the back of the spool and spools with profiled centres, which ensure you will get an even, level lay to the line on the spool (*see* Fig 6). Many of the later reels, particularly those produced by Shimano, have multiple drag control systems which allow a number of pre-determined settings to be employed to suit the circumstances. There is a 'strike' setting which allows for firm hook setting and a normal midway point of clutch slip. There is a light (minimum setting) on one

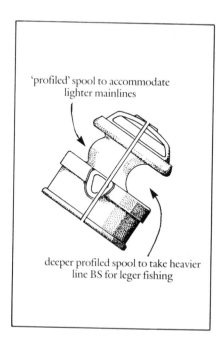

'profiled' spool to accommodate lighter mainlines

deeper profiled spool to take heavier line BS for leger fishing

Fig 6   Spool profiles.

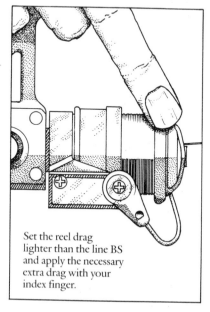

Set the reel drag lighter than the line BS and apply the necessary extra drag with your index finger.

Fig 7   Applying finger pressure to a reel spool.

side which can be selected at a flick to give line to a bolting fish, control being applied by finger pressure to the spool (*see* Fig 7), and finally, a maximum setting on the other side which would allow the angler to apply pressure to slow a running fish and eventually hold it from snags etc.

The Right Reel

Choosing the correct reel can be difficult and listed here are some of the more useful reels with line capacities and so on. Again, you will find that quality is commensurate with cost, but a compromise can be struck with reels more easily than with rods. The best advice is to take a long hard look at as many as is possible and not to just follow fashion – buy one that meets all your requirements.

Centre Pins

Moving away from the high-technology of today's fixed spool reels, there is a strong upsurge in interest in the centre pin reels, probably as a result of the exposure given to it by John Wilson in many of his television programmes in the *Go Fishing* series. John has spent a lot of his angling career developing his skills with a centre pin and he is most certainly an expert. He makes it look so easy. In fact, it will take a lot of practice to overcome the fixed spool bias.

That said, there can be no better way of presenting a stickfloat than with a centre pin reel. The important point with choosing one is to obtain the right type for your circumstance. Very few are manufactured now, although it seems that one or two individual manufacturers

John Wilson long trotting on the River Kennet.

Prepared for a day's roving along the River Wissey.

Make and Model	Ratio	Spool Capacity
Diawa Carbon SF1350TM	3.7:1	100m × 2lb BS
Diawa Harrier 1657DM	5.4:1	110m × 4lb BS
Shimano SMN-M-2500X	5.2:1	120m × 2lb BS
Shimano Leger Spool		250m × 6lb BS
Shimano SSG-X 1000	5.2:1	165m × 4lb BS
Dam CFM Match	4.1:1	100m × 3lb BS
Dam Leger Spool		200m × 8lb BS
Ryobi ML3	5.1:1	110m × 4lb BS
Ryobi Leger Spool		250m × 6lb BS

Table 3   Reels.

have gone back into production on a limited number basis, to cater for the new demand. Unfortunately these reels are not cheap, so choose wisely.

LINES

Choice of line is equally, if not more, important as the choice of rod and reel. If you choose the wrong line for a given situation and there is no balance between the action of the rod and the line breaking strain, you will risk breakage and disappointment either during the cast, on the strike, during the fight or should the fish bolt at the net.

Matched to Test Curves

All of this can be avoided by careful matching of line strengths to test curves. You can get away with exceeding the rod's maximum recommended line breaking strain, but you will not find much forgiveness for going below its minimum – choose carefully.

Quality Line

Listed in Table 4 are some quality, proven makes of both main lines and suitable hook length lines for use when lighter diameter lines may be necessary to catch line-shy fish. Many of the specialised hooklink lines are more expensive than the bulk-spooled main lines like Sylcast or Maxima, etc. so it makes sense to fill your spools with one of these brands, storing hooklinks in smaller quantities for use as required. An important point to bear in mind, with all lines, is to put adequate line on to the reel spool to allow easy casting, but not excessive amounts that will easily spill off before, or prematurely during, the cast. You can see the correct level of line on a spool in Fig 8. If hook links are lighter than the reel line, they should

Make	Strength/BS	Diameter
Drennan Specimen	1½lb–0.70kg	0.125mm
Drennan Specimen	2½lb–1.13kg	0.150mm
Drennan Specimen	3lb–1.35kg	0.175mm
Drennan Floatfish	3–2lb–1.45kg	0.175mm
Drennan Floatfish	1–1lb–0.45kg	0.100mm
Drennan Floatfish	1.7lb–0.77kg	0.125mm
Drennan Floatfish	5lb–2.25kg	0.225mm
Maxima Chameleon	1lb–0.05kg	0.080mm
Maxima Chameleon	2lb–1.00kg	0.120mm
Maxima Chameleon	3lb–1.40kg	0.150mm
Maxima Chameleon	5lb–2.40kg	0.200mm
Sylcast Sorrel	1lb–0.50kg	0.080mm
Sylcast Sorrel	1½lb–0.70kg	0.090mm
Sylcast Sorrel	3lb–1.35kg	0.100mm
Sylcast Sorrel	4lb–1.80kg	0.170mm
Sylcast Sorrel	5lb–2.25kg	0.200mm

Table 4   Lines.

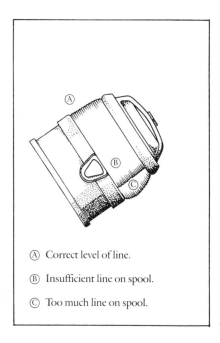

(A) Correct level of line.

(B) Insufficient line on spool.

(C) Too much line on spool.

Fig 8   Correct line level on a reel spool.

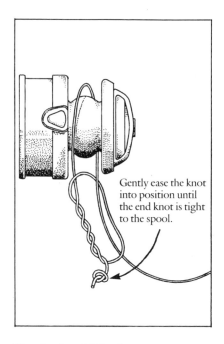

Gently ease the knot into position until the end knot is tight to the spool.

Fig 9   Spool fixing knot.

be at least eighteen inches long, if possible, to allow there to be some degree of stretch within its length to avoid breakage. This acts as a shock absorber!

KNOTS

An important point to remember with nylon monofilament line is that it will only be as strong as its weakest point which is usually the knot. Ensure you get the optimum knot strength. Some useful and practical knots appear in Figs 9, 10, 11, 12 and 13. Great care should be taken when tying all your knots and it is important that they should all be moistened prior to being fully tightened. Do not rush the tightening – take your time and you will get a stronger finish. Remember, it can make the difference between landing and losing that leviathan.

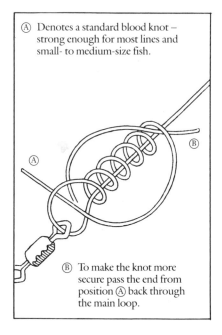

(A) Denotes a standard blood knot – strong enough for most lines and small- to medium-size fish.

(B) To make the knot more secure pass the end from position (A) back through the main loop.

Fig 10   Plain and tucked blood knot.

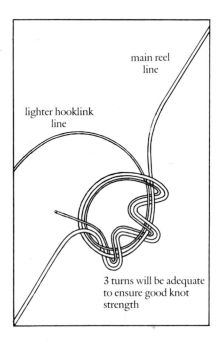

main reel
line

lighter hooklink
line

3 turns will be adequate
to ensure good knot
strength

Fig 11   Water knot.

TERMINAL TACKLES

Whilst lines, rods and reels are important for remaining in contact with a hooked fish, the terminal tackles we choose to actually hook our quarry with are of paramount import Choose the wrong terminal tackle combina tion and bites may go unnoticed, or worse still result in deep hookings. The ability to balance all the components, down to the terminal tackle, will go a long way to ensuring the reward of having a fairly hooked fish on the bank.

Versatile Swivel

Moving down the line, some of the most important components are going to be good swivels and illustrated in Fig 14 are three of the many types available. Of the three, the most versatile is the centre one, the 'Diamond Eye' available from Drennan Tackle. Also shown are some of the snap links that are available for use

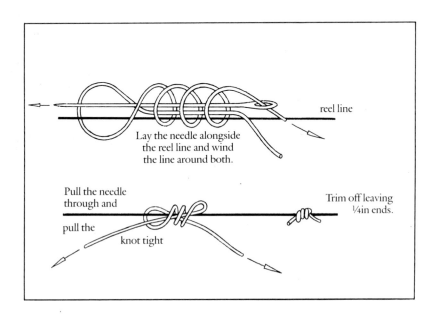

reel line

Lay the needle alongside
the reel line and wind
the line around both.

Pull the needle
through and

pull the

knot tight

Trim off leaving
¼in ends.

Fig 12   Needle formed stop-knot.

Mike Woods quiver-tipping on the River Yare.

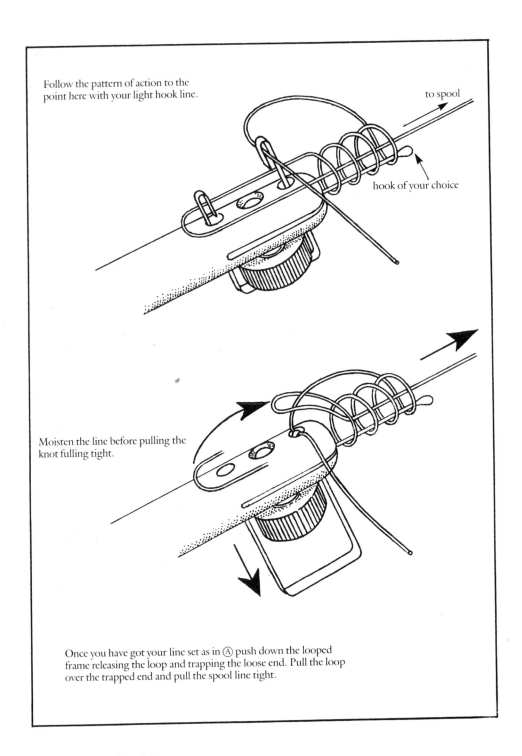

Follow the pattern of action to the point here with your light hook line.

to spool

hook of your choice

Moisten the line before pulling the knot fulling tight.

Once you have got your line set as in Ⓐ push down the looped frame releasing the loop and trapping the loose end. Pull the loop over the trapped end and pull the spool line tight.

Fig 13   Spade end hook knot.

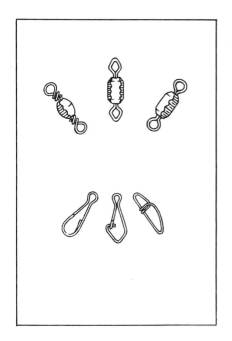

Fig 14   Assorted swivels and link clips.

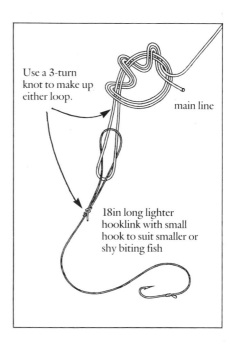

Use a 3-turn knot to make up either loop.

main line

18in long lighter hooklink with small hook to suit smaller or shy biting fish

Fig 15   Looped light hooklinks fixing.

with the illustrated swivels. The centre one, the Drennan 'Safeloc', is very useful and reliable for attaching paternoster links or leger weights, and swim feeders, etc. Swivels can be used, as will be seen in the methods sections, for sliding links, terminating the reel line and joining the hook links.

Hook Links

The hook links, which will be of the same breaking strain through to the hook or lighter, can be joined by twin loops or as a fixed pater-noster by using the water knot (*see* Figs 11 and 15). Without swivels and heavy weights it is possible to use plastic leger stops like those marketed by Drennan Tackle and Gardner Tackle. These can be used with small brass rings as shown in Fig 61, to which a nylon link and SSG weights can be added when light balanced legering is required.

HOOKS

When it comes to choosing hooks, you will probably build up confidence in a particular make and pattern, usually because of a bad experience or disappointment with another make. This addiction to one hook is very common, but many of the serious anglers who were once committed in this way have found that the development of specialised carp hooks has given us a wide range of hooks which suit certain species other than carp. These have improved the capture ratio in our favour (*see* Fig 16).

Chemical Etching

Probably the single most important advance has been the chemical etching of the points to a sharpness once only dreamt of. There is one shortcoming, however – the points are very

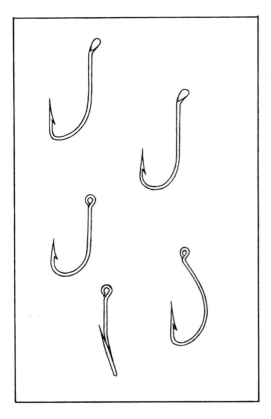

Fig 16   Hook bend and fixing patterns.

easily damaged when fishing near stony areas or where hard snags exist. It pays to check the point regularly and if it is damaged, change the hook.

The second great advance is the development of fully closed eyes. No longer is there the risk of the line getting trapped or even cut in the gap, once common on many hook eyes. Many of the smaller baits now have hooks designed for them, in particular, caster hooks for complete concealment of the hook within the caster.

Hook Choice

Bait presentation will probably dictate the hook type and size you will choose. Baits fully mounted on the hook such as luncheon meat or bread and cheese pastes will require a hook with a fairly wide gape, whilst off-hook or hair-type presentations may require smaller, turned in pointed hooks. You will probably form a preference in due course but you will find a selection of reliable brands and patterns listed in Table 5.

Make	Model	Specification	Sizes
Mustad	Blue Match	Spade End Long Shank	16, 18, 20
Drennan	Long Match	Spade End Long Shank	16, 18, 20
Drennan	Carbon Feeder	Offset Curved Point Spade End	10, 12, 14, 16, 18, 20
Drennan	Carbon Caster	Long Shank Crystal Bend Spade End	16, 18, 20
Drennan	Carbon Specimen	Eyed Curved Point	2 through to 18
Drennan	Super Specialist	Eyed	2 through to 20

Table 5   Hooks.

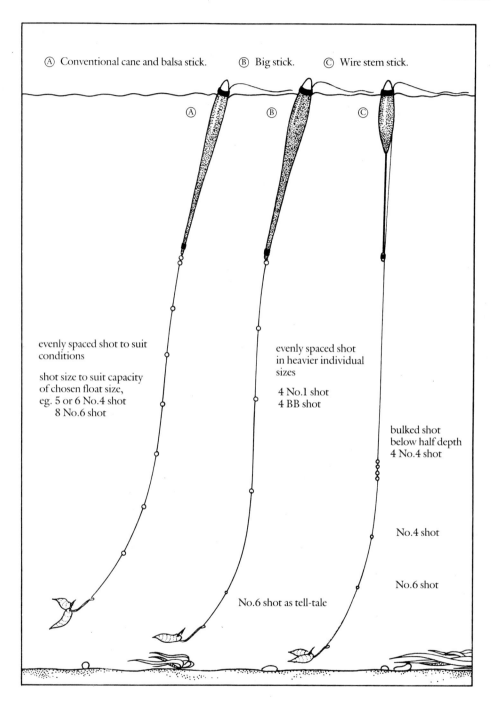

Fig 17   Assorted stickfloats and shotting patterns.

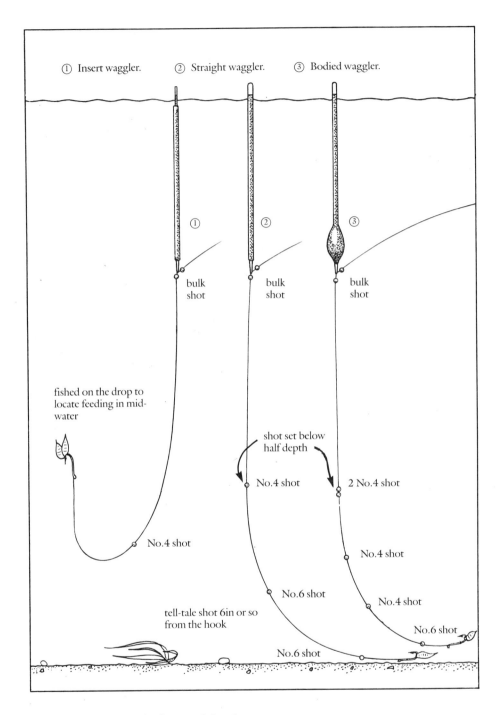

Fig 18   Assorted waggler floats and shotting patterns.

FLOATS

It is probably true to say that more anglers are caught by floats than fish. Look in any angler's tackle box and you will find more floats than he ever uses. We all fall into the same trap at some time. It is good advice to control your urges and keep a few practical ones, learning how to use them properly.

Illustrated in Figs 17, 18 and 19 are a selection of useful floats for running water. Full details of how to use them can be found in the methods section, where shotting patterns are also shown to suit various situations.

SWIM FEEDERS

An important component in fishing running water, the swim feeder helps get bait down to the bottom quickly and accurately, ensuring that the hook bait is right where the groundbait is. There are many different styles and a selection of the most useful ones are shown in Fig 20, from block-end maggot only feeders, to open-end and mesh feeders. It is worth arming yourself with a selection of these in the sizes that will suit your tackle. It is no use having swim feeders that will weigh three ounces when full, if your rod and line can only handle two ounces for casting – something is bound to break.

ROD RESTS

You will require a selection of rod rests and shown in Figs 21 and 22 are some of the more suitable rod rest heads which will be very practical in use. A good selection of non-toxic split shot and leger weights, from approximately an eighth of an ounce up to one-and-half ounces, will cover most circumstances.

I could continue covering items of tackle in this chapter but it would probably be more useful to cover some of the other items, in detail, in the methods chapters.

TRAVEL LIGHT

We all accumulate items that we like to use as individuals, but it is worth mentioning here that when fishing running water it is more practical to keep the tackle you carry down to a minimum. Too much will see you worn out from carrying it over long distances. Travelling light will encourage you to move to a fresh swim when bites are slow or actually stop. This will probably see you catching more fish and gaining a wider experience of the chosen water.

Equip yourself with a small rucksack or

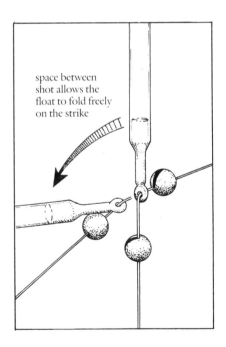

space between shot allows the float to fold freely on the strike

Fig 19   Waggler float fixing with bulkshot.

The action of a good quiver-tip rod.

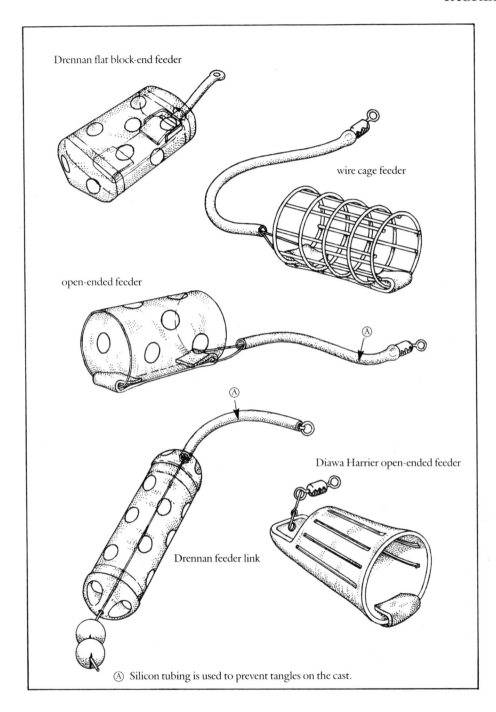

Fig 20   Selection of useful swimfeeders.

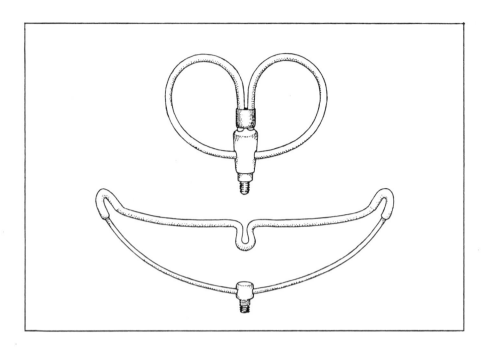

Fig 21   Useful float rod rests.

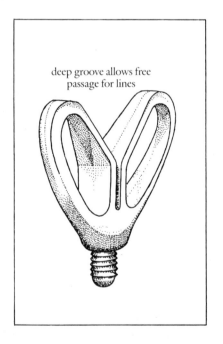

deep groove allows free
passage for lines

Fig 22   Drennan rubber rod rest.

tackle bag and a small folding stool, not a big
cavernous tackle box and a garden chair, which
will make you too comfortable to keep on the
move. Another useful item is a small tackle
quiver which will hold a couple of rod rests,
maybe an umbrella and your landing net – a
full rod bag will just be a nuisance.

3 Baits

Depending on their views and the nature of their interest in fishing running water, be it pleasure or specimen oriented, different people will tend towards different baits. What these baits all have in common is that they give the angler a confidence that grows the more often they use their particular choice.

PERSONAL CHOICE

There will be anglers who use their favourite choice of bait no matter which species they are fishing for. This familiarity with the bait gives him confidence. Whilst some of the suggestions of just what bait you should use for each species may be correct, this could be as a result of the particular bait or baits having been used exclusively on a given water. There is nothing to say that an alternative choice could not catch fish in the same location, particularly if it is used correctly and confidently.

Fishing on running water, be it on small upper, non-tidal reaches of river or the larger tidal stretches, is very much akin to stillwater fishing in that styles and, more importantly here, baits come into fashion from time to time. This often happens when large catches or individual large fish are caught and publicised by the captor. Greater weight is added to this if the angler in question is a noted match or specialist angler.

The bait used may have been an ordinary one, that we all use from time to time and it is quite possible that the next time it is used, the results will be different, particularly if the bait

has been used extensively and the fish have become wise to it. Fish soon recognise which bait is safe and they learn to avoid the one with the hook in it.

Super Baits

Many secret additives exist, mainly in anglers' minds, and many so-called magic mixes of attractors appear, for sale, for the many fish-hungry anglers to add to their baits. There are some comparisons with carp fishing here, in that it is very easy to become preoccupied with the smell or colour of the particular bait you use. Some of the additives may work. We have all tried adding something to make our bait better or at least a bit different, and if it helps to catch, then it strengthens confidence, leaving time to concentrate more on presentation or location. However, remember that if you start using Bloggs 'Barbel Booster' additive, it is possible that every other angler is doing the same and you might just as well be fishing simple maggot or bread.

Be Different

To summarise, it is highly likely that the big catch or big fish that inspired you was caught, not because of a super bait, but because the angler tried something new or at least something different to what everybody else was using. The moral is, try and learn what everybody else is using and then try something better or at least different. It may be that only slightly better quality bait will be necessary. If

Loading an open-end swimfeeder with maggots.

you fish with a quality bait in the right place, at the right time, you will stand more of a chance of catching than if you follow somebody else's lead. By the time it is publicised, it is already too late.

Quality Baits

Accepting that you wish to be successful at catching whatever it is your sights are set on, be it lots of small to medium-size fish or fewer medium-size to large specimens, then the most important thing to remember is that the bait you use must be of the highest quality. It is no good just accepting that a bait catches because it is what it is; some baits have a peak level of attraction and to use them in any other condition will prove fruitless, even to the point that the fish may be repelled.

Many a tale has been told of the angler who cannot catch using a simple bait like bread or

maggot whilst his near neighbour is pulling fish out, one after the other. It is possible that the bait of the successful angler is at its peak of condition. His maggots are kept in clean bran and are sweet and attractive to the fish, whilst the other angler is using sweaty, smelly, stale maggots, bought from a supplier who only sells maggots because he has to! It is far better to buy from a source where care is taken over storage and cleanliness (more on this subject as we progress).

Confidence

Hopefully you will be able to see that there is a need to give more thought to your bait than perhaps you have before. You will be surprised how much knowing you are using the best quality bait will do for your confidence and success, whichever species you are after.

What follows in the remainder of this

chapter is a range of successful baits and details of how to get them to their best condition as necessary. This will include hook baits and groundbaits (the latter can be as important to success as the hook bait).

MAGGOTS

Maggots are available everywhere, easy to use and will catch almost every species of fish that swims in a lake or river! The fact that all this is true leads to a lot of misuse of maggots and, likewise, a lot of disappointment. The humble maggot, in one of its three forms – the large white, the pinkie or the squatt – is so readily available that many anglers pop into their nearest tackle dealer and purchase a half-pint or one pint of whichever maggot is available! In many cases these will be plain white or a mix of white and coloured maggots. The angler will then proceed to go fishing the same day or the following day with what he presumes is a good bait. He will not give a thought to their condition, other than to comment if they smell badly!

Dealer Attitude

The maggot is an excellent bait, but the quality of a shop-bought supply will depend on the dealer's attitude to his bait. If he has no interest in angling and the shop operates in some other capacity as well as fishing tackle, it is unlikely that time will be available for bait care. The bait will probably be stored in a fridge in the same medium in which it was supplied from the maggot farm (invariably sawdust). The maggots will become very smelly and contaminated which will undoubtedly deter fish from taking them when offered on the hook (*see* Fig 23). Also, some of the maggots will be old and they may start to turn to casters within hours of buying.

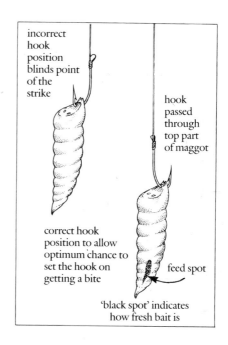

Fig 23   Maggots on the hook.

If the maggots are purchased from a good-quality tackle dealer who sets out to supply a good service to anglers, both in tackle and bait, he will take the trouble to set up a proper system of bait care. This will start with cleaning off the sawdust in which the maggots were supplied, using a vibrating riddle. The cleaned maggots will then be placed in clean trays and ground maize added to further clean and freshen them. They will be refrigerated until sold. Whilst in store, intermittent turning and riddling continues to remove any dead maggots, skins or casters. At the point of sale, the bait will be topped up with ground maize to keep it clean and fresh.

Match Anglers

If at all possible, you should locate a bait supplier that is like the latter. Match anglers will usually frequent a better dealer, so, if you can, ask where they get their maggots from. If you cannot find a good supplier or distance prohibits using one, then you will have to make do with the 'dirty' local supply and take some steps towards bringing the bait up to standard. There is no question of it being necessary or not – if you really wish to be successful at catching fish of any species, your bait must be of the highest possible quality.

If you opt for using the local supply, be it dirty, moderate or first-class, there is one exercise which will improve them all. Only the degree will vary from source to source. Assuming that you have to buy from the local corner shop which sells maggots, it will be worth finding out how many gallons of maggots are used weekly and what frequency of supply the dealer has! Once you find a shop that gets a weekly supply, find out on which day the bait arrives and buy your bait as soon after that day as possible. A good fresh maggot will have a black feed spot visible through the skin. Maggots without this may be quite old.

Clean and Prepare your Own

If you have fresh maggots, riddle them clean of the sawdust or whatever they were supplied in, with a riddle tray (*see* Fig 24), by shaking the tray briskly over a large container. Recover any maggots that drop through and then tip all of them into a bowl containing ground maize or dampened bran and allow them half an hour to wriggle and clean themselves. Repeat the process again, putting the maggots into fresh dry bran and then place them in the fridge to keep them cool. It is important not to put too many maggots into a bait box. If in doubt, use two boxes! The bait needs room to breathe; too many maggots squashed into a box will sweat and become smelly. In the case of the better bait supply, a change from the original maize to fresh maize or bran will help keep it in top condition. Make a habit of cleaning your

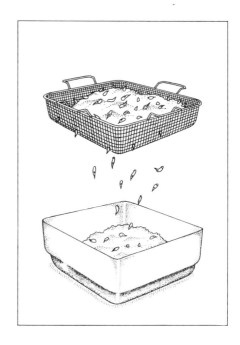

Fig 24　Riddle tray in use.

bait when you buy it and you will gain an edge on the anglers who do not.

Coloured Bait

Coloured maggots are best purchased ready-dyed. The professional colouring is stronger and costs no more anyway. Red, bronze and pink are the most popular colours after white. More on colour in the appropriate chapters.

CASTERS

For many species, casters can be a superior bait, but they have to be just right. Like maggots, if they are not at their peak of attraction and quality, they will be rejected. For many years the caster was discarded as useless by anglers who used maggots as baits.

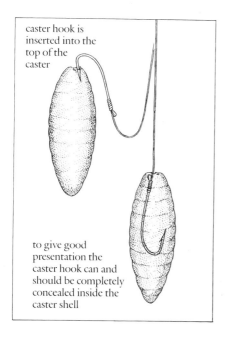

caster hook is inserted into the top of the caster

to give good presentation the caster hook can and should be completely concealed inside the caster shell

Fig 25   Casters on the hook.

However, when a high percentage of maggots turned to casters just before and during the day of fishing, the casters in the loose feed had the effect of conditioning the fish to feed on casters instead of maggots. Fish could be seen feeding but not on hook baits. It was discovered that casters sank at certain stages in their development and that if the supply of casters were at this stage, then feeding with loose caster and hooking single caster carefully could produce bumper bags as the fish (all species), became preoccupied with a delicious bait (*see* Fig 25).

Top-quality casters can be obtained from 'good' tackle dealers, the operative word being 'good', because to produce good-quality casters it requires the continuous care and interest of the dealer to riddle off casters several times a day to ensure they are collected and stored in peak conditions. This is too

much for many tackle shops, but the ability to supply good-quality caster will ensure the tackle dealer gains good trade from regular customers. It will pay to locate a good source and use it regularly.

Home-Produced Casters

It is possible to produce casters at home. We all do it to some degree, by accident sometimes. The difficulty is producing the quantity we may need at exactly the right moment. If you wish to do so, the important point to remember is to purchase fresh maggots with a feed spot visible. This will ensure that the bait is fresh from the bait breeder! Ensure that you have bait of one age – some dealers may supply bait of mixed supplies which will mean casters being produced over several days instead of within several hours.

The secret to turning casters is to allow them space and air to breathe and to keep turning them to ensure they all get exposed to the warmth of the environment. The warmer the place of storage, the quicker the caster will turn, but do not be tempted to speed this up by using excessive heat. Equally, the cooler it is, the slower the turning will be. If you have taken into consideration the age of your maggot supply, you will get a fairly even turn from maggot to caster. If this is so, all you will need to do is periodically riddle the maggots that are still alive through a proper mesh riddle tray (*see* Fig 24).

As the casters are obtained, they should be placed into polythene bags from which the air is then cleared by gently squeezing and tying the bag tight. These can then be kept in the bottom of the fridge. Good casters will be a golden bronze colour but any caster lighter in colour will be ideal for storage. The dark ruby coloured ones are usually no good because they will float – check by dropping them in water if you are unsure!

HEMP SEED

Powerful Attractor

Whilst an excellent hook bait, the real use for hemp seed with most anglers today is as an attractor for just about every species in our rivers. This may be loose feed placed into the swim by hand, catapult, bait dropper or swim feeder. Hemp seed attracts by sight and smell and will usually draw and hold fish in a swim allowing an alternative bait to be offered directly amongst the bed of hemp. An example of this is the use of luncheon meat over hemp for chub and barbel. The hemp acts as the attractor, preoccupying the fish which then take the meat-baited hook.

Natural Oils

There is a theory that, when properly cooked, hemp seed resembles a snail and when presented in large quantities, it resembles a natural bed of snails. Whether this is true or not will be for you to ponder, but one thing is certain – the sight of the white inner flesh of the cooked and split hemp seed is very attractive visually and the smell of the natural oil released from the cooked hemp presents a pleasing scent. The small white tail may aid the visual attraction.

Cooking Hemp

The preparation of hemp seed is very simple. Pre-soaking for a few hours will be beneficial but the seed can be cooked straight from the bag by placing a pint of it in a saucepan with two pints of water. Bring this to the boil and then leave it to simmer for as long as it takes to open the shell of the seed and release the white inner flesh (approximately fifteen to twenty minutes). Once this is complete, the hemp seed is ready for use either as an attractor or hook bait. Allow the bait to cool in its own juices and retain the liquid for use in groundbait or as a liquid attractor which can be poured into the swim, at intervals, to increase the attractor levels. Alternatively, you can freeze this liquid into blocks in an ice cube tray. You can then attach these to a leger weight with a piece of thread frozen into the blocks, or freeze a stone in the cube to make them sink quickly.

Flask-Cooked Hemp

The second method for preparing hemp is in a flask. Place your hemp (maybe a pint), into a large two-pint vacuum flask and then pour in enough boiling water to leave a small space at the top. Replace the cap and leave for six to eight hours, overnight, and when you open the flask the hemp seed should be suitably cooked and ready for use.

Ground Hemp

In addition to cooked hemp seed being useful as an attractor and bait, it can be very useful to use ground uncooked hemp seed in your groundbait mix. The natural oils are released along with the ground seed generating a high level of attraction. Indeed, many commercial groundbaits include it in reasonable quantities. The addition of this form of hemp seed into your own mix could prove very rewarding.

Hemp on the Hook

The art of using hemp seed as hookbait is to mount it either on the hook as a single grain or on a hair or hairs as a multiple-grain presentation. The various methods can be seen in Figs 26 and 27. It will obviously depend on which species you are after. Single grains would be ideal for roach with a fine wire hook of size 16

Good chub taken on a natural bait – slug.

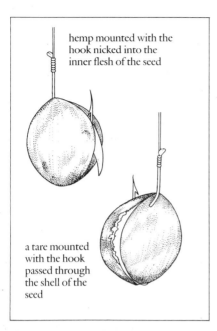

hemp mounted with the hook nicked into the inner flesh of the seed

a tare mounted with the hook passed through the shell of the seed

Fig 26   Hemp and tares mounted on the hook.

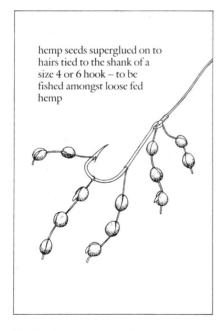

hemp seeds superglued on to hairs tied to the shank of a size 4 or 6 hook – to be fished amongst loose fed hemp

Fig 27   Hemp mounted on hair-rigged hook.

or 18 whilst multiple baits on hairs would be suitable for larger species like chub or barbel.

TARES

The minute size of hemp seed makes hooking tedious and there are some alternatives. One is to use one of the commercially made imitation hemp seeds which you never need to change or re-bait! The second is to use tares for hookbaits instead. The tares are slightly larger and are softer in texture, once cooked, making presentation and hooking far better (*see* Fig 26).

Preparing Tares

You should cook tares in the same way as you would hemp seed except that you can add a pinch of bicarbonate of soda to help them retain the black colour normally lost during cooking. Add two pints of water to a pint of tares and leave them to soak (overnight if possible). There is less in the way of a natural attractor, in the form of oil, in tares so it could prove useful to add your own. The liquid flavours used in carp baits can be used to great effect. The addition of these, after cooking, can be useful. Hemp seed and maple flavourings are ideal.

Once soaked, place the tares in a saucepan and bring to the boil. Leave them to simmer for fifteen to twenty minutes but check the bait regularly after ten minutes. Cooking in a vacuum flask works reasonably well but the saucepan is more efficient. Allow the bait to cool in its own juices and drain when cold.

BREAD BAITS

Probably the first bait we all use and the premier bait for just about every species we may fish for in our rivers is bread. The most

...sed and undoubtedly the most abused means of presenting a bread bait is bread flake. If it is not presented correctly it will not be accepted and even if it is accepted, the hook will be shielded and unable to find a hold when striking at a bite.

Flake Texture

Good presentation begins with the type of bread chosen as the hook bait. The premier bread is not always a fresh uncut loaf, although some such loaves can be superb. For convenience and consistency in quality, a fresh cut loaf from the supermarket is probably the best buy. For flake to be really effective, the way it is placed on the hook is very important (*see* Fig 28). The most important points to remember are: do not mask the point of the hook thus obscuring the chance of finding a hookhold

when a bite comes and make sure that the bread flake is firmly attached. This is where the moist texture of the supermarket cut loaf comes in – it allows a light pinch to obtain a good hold but is not so stiff that it will not come off on the strike or on the retrieve. If the bait comes back on the retrieve it is too firm and therefore no good.

Crust Texture

Crust, either floating or anchored on the bottom, is the next most useful of baits taken from a loaf of bread (*see* Fig 29). This bait should be taken from a freshly baked crusty loaf. The moist crust of a supermarket cut loaf will not do. Probably the best loaf to use is a sandwich loaf which has a large area of white, medium-textured crust. This can be cut into small, finger-nail sized cubes for bottom pre-

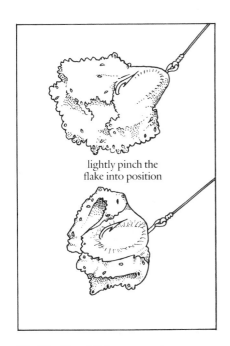

lightly pinch the
flake into position

Fig 28 Bread flake mounted on the hook.

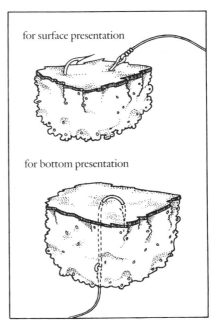

for surface presentation

for bottom presentation

Fig 29 Bread crust on the hook.

A fine 4lb-plus chub on cheese paste for Mike Woods.

sentation or almost matchbox sized pieces for surface presentation for chub.

Surface crust can be fished on a free-line basis to allow the bait to drift into the snaggy holding areas of overhanging roots and brambles and alongside weed rafts. Ensure that you use a greased line, though, to make the bait move along with the current.

CHEESE

Diced Cheese

Cheese is a very effective bait, particularly for catching chub, although barbel and roach take it as well. Very few people use cheese as a bait, having no confidence in it. Those who do, know its value, particularly in conditions when the river is carrying some colour and it can be located by smell. Cheddar, Edam and Red Leicester all offer a fine, easy-to-produce chunky bait, cut from the block as bought.

Grated Cheese

An alternative way to use cheese is by grating it down and mixing it with flour and water. This allows a softer cheese paste to be made up for when the water temperature is at its lowest, thereby ensuring that the hook presentation is at its best.

To effect the mixing of this type of paste, grate your chosen cheese and add a small quantity of flour, then water (added in small amounts), and mix until a firm, doughy paste is obtained. This soft paste can be moulded on the hook and small cubes of the original cheese can be diced off to be fed into the swim as free offerings (*see* Fig 30).

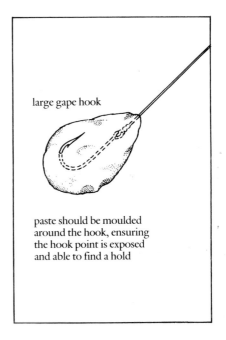

large gape hook

paste should be moulded around the hook, ensuring the hook point is exposed and able to find a hold

Fig 30 Soft pastes on the hook.

PASTES

Another bait suitable for many species is a bread-based paste. This may include cheese or any other additive that can be mixed with the bread. Cheese is probably the most used and there are various recipes for mixing a good cheese paste, many of which you can experiment with, to come up with your own special mix.

Paste Mixing

The simplest way to mix a paste is to take four or five slices of freshly cut loaf and trim off all the crusts. Then take a cheese spread like Primula, either in its original flavour or with ham or mixed seafood added, and spread a thick layer over each slice of bread. Lay one slice on top of another and then squeeze and knead the lot together to make a smooth, even-textured bait. The paste may stiffen in cold water so the hooking should take this into account allowing an easy shedding of the bait from the hook, when striking to hook the fish (*see* Fig 30).

Attractive Flake

The addition of this same spread to bread flake can also improve the catch rate on days when little seems to respond to flake on its own. Simply spread the cheese over the flake prior to casting. An enticing trail of dissolving spread will drift downstream from the bait, drawing the fish upstream towards it.

LUNCHEON MEAT

Luncheon meat is one of the most successful baits, particularly where chub and barbel are concerned. It has given many anglers the opportunity to catch their biggest specimens of either species. If either chub or barbel are present in a stretch of river, luncheon meat will usually entice them. It's not the super bait but it is one that seems to attract and deceive the fish time and again.

Avoiding Problems with Luncheon Meat

Whilst the more expensive varieties of luncheon meat offer higher meat contents and possibly higher flavour levels, they can prove difficult to use on the hook, as they are usually very soft. The cheaper brands contain more fat and milk product, such as caseinate, which tends to make them more solid and, therefore, more stable for hooking. A brand that contains large lumps of meat or gristle is best not used for hook baits as these may impede the strike if the bait is hook-mounted (*see* Fig 31), however they may be ideal for hair rigging. High-fat luncheon meat can prove difficult in warm weather as it becomes loose and oily, but it is possible to overcome this by making a paste using breadcrumbs to stiffen the meat and then moulding the paste on to the hook. Another way is to allow the bait to skin over by allowing it to lie exposed to the air and sun. This tends to make it tough and leathery which is ideal for hooking.

Reliable Brands of Luncheon Meat

You will find many varieties of tinned meat on the shelves of the supermarket and corner store. Some seem to be more attractive than others. Spam, Plumrose and Bacon Grill are to be strongly recommended, but experiment to find one that you can use easily and which the fish like (*see* Fig 31).

WORMS

The worm is a natural bait, readily taken by many species in its various forms, from the small red worm to the largest lob worm. The biggest problem with worms, for most anglers who want to give them a try, is actually collecting and keeping them. The best way of accumulating lob worms is to catch them, direct from the lawn, after dark. Red worms can be found in the soft soil and leaf moulds in any wooded areas of ground. To keep worms fresh and, therefore, at their best, keep them in a bait tub filled with fresh, damp moss and peat, or just damp peat alone.

Alternative Baits

Lob worms can be used whole, with the hook passed through the 'collar' or even in pieces. The most useful piece is the tail section (*see* Fig 33). The larger species will accept the lob worm whole whilst it may be necessary to

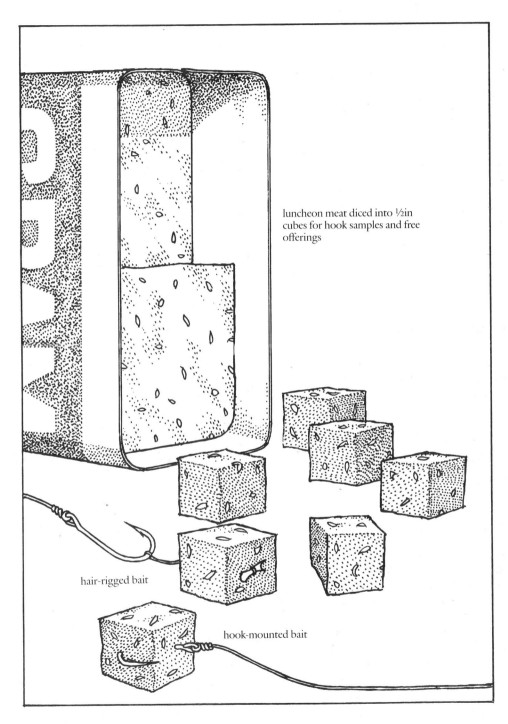

luncheon meat diced into ½in cubes for hook samples and free offerings

hair-rigged bait

hook-mounted bait

Fig 31   Luncheon meat on the hook and hair rigged.

Surprise is around every bend – a good brown trout.

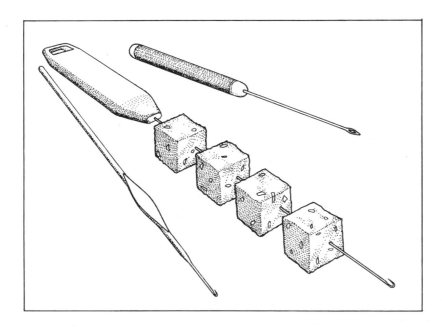

Fig 32   Assorted baiting needles.

5lb chub caught on flake coated with soft cheese.

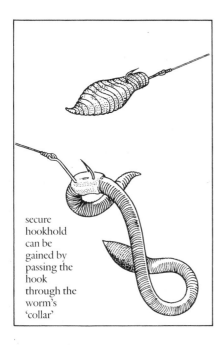

secure hookhold can be gained by passing the hook through the worm's 'collar'

Fig 33   Lobworm and lobtail on the hook.

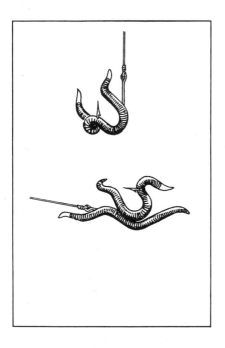

Fig 34   Redworm mounted on the hook.

resort to single or double red worms to tempt roach and bream etc. (*see* Fig 34). For those who are not able to obtain a good supply of worms at home, most tackle dealers stock containers of small red worms.

That covers just about all of the most useful and productive baits. Other baits do exist – just about any edible item could possibly catch fish. The best move would be to get a few fish on the bank and then try some of the alternatives if you so wish. Several of the paste bait mixes used by carp and tench anglers hold some potential for chub, barbel and bream. Some of the flavourings have very effective powers of attraction for certain species and these can be added to your ordinary baits if necessary. The important thing is to match the bait to the situation. More often than not a very basic, simple bait will be more effective than a complex one, so try the simple option first!

GROUNDBAITS

The choice of groundbaits will be down to individual preference. Walk into any good tackle dealer and on display will be a large variety of good-quality groundbait mixes from one of the reputable manufacturers – British Groundbaits, Sensas and Marcel Van Den Eynde, to list but a few. These are well-proven mixes aimed at particular types of fisheries, as well as specific fish! Many are based on successful continental recipes using herbs, hemp and many other specialised ingredients for attraction, binding and other qualities.

Additives

The importance of groundbaits and groundbaiting is to draw and hold your target species. Additives and specialised mixes will be necessary at some point but it is very easy to get tied up in bait mixes and forget the fish.

It is more important to master the practicalities of how to mix and use groundbait, than to get involved too deeply with the contents of a groundbait mixture. Groundbait contents should complement the hookbait, for example, when you use bread flake the ideal groundbait will be mashed bread.

Mashed Bread

Mashed bread is simplicity itself in that you only need a small amount of stale bread (a sliced loaf left open for a couple of days will fit the bill). This is simply soaked, at the waterside, in a bowl or in the mesh of the landing-net and then the excess water is poured or squeezed out. This leaves a mushy, loose mix that can be introduced into the swim in small quantities, for pre-baiting and groundbaiting. Because it is light and buoyant it can also be used to indicate the current action on a stretch of river.

Breadcrumb

Moving on to ready-prepared bait, the most widely used is probably breadcrumbs. You can buy breadcrumbs in packs from 2lb up to 50lb and in white, brown or golden forms. On their own, breadcrumbs constitute a basic feed for loose feeding and for swimfeeder plugging. However, many additives can be used with them, including the proprietary mixes from home and continental suppliers, the choice of which I will leave up to you.

Mixing Groundbaits

More important than recommending specific mixes is describing the way to mix groundbaits to suit the circumstances of the fishery. A lot of the secrets of your venues will be learnt only by experimenting on them yourself. However, I can point out some basic ground rules.

Groundbait Texture

There are many things that come together to make the use of groundbait successful – knowing what quantity of fish you may be fishing amongst, what the river condition is and where the fish will be. Too much feed, in the form of groundbait, will not only draw and hold your quarry but also overfeed them, and, therefore, reduce your opportunity to get them to take a hookbait. If the mixing is too stiff or too loose, it may lie on the bottom in a firm ball for too long and not actually attract any fish, or it might break up, on entry, and come to settle one hundred yards (100m) downstream of where you are fishing, taking the fish with it (see Fig 35).

The same situation occurs with the use of breadcrumbs to plug open-end feeders and cage feeders – too firm a mix and it will not release the bait samples; too loose and it will break up on entry, drawing the fish away.

General Attractor

The optimum groundbait will respond to the circumstances. A bottom bait should not break up until it sits on the bottom when it should break up slowly and spread out to be carried downstream on the current, drawing the fish up to the baited swim! A general attractor, cloud-type bait should break up progressively as it falls through the water, so offering a wide band of small bait particles over the river bed, again leading up to the main swim.

The Right Quantity

Groundbaits must be mixed to suit the swim and the method. They must be of the right quantity to suit the fish population – attract-

A good chub falls to a simple bait – breadflake.

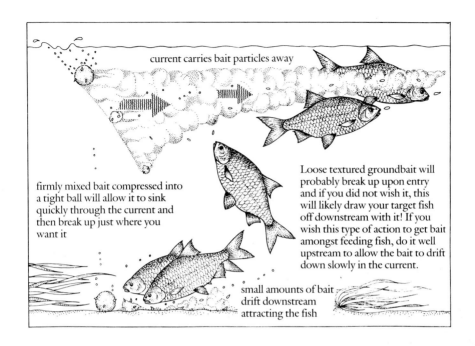

current carries bait particles away

firmly mixed bait compressed into a tight ball will allow it to sink quickly through the current and then break up just where you want it

Loose textured groundbait will probably break up upon entry and if you did not wish it, this will likely draw your target fish off downstream with it! If you wish this type of action to get bait amongst feeding fish, do it well upstream to allow the bait to drift down slowly in the current.

small amounts of bait drift downstream attracting the fish

Fig 35 Groundbait action in the swim.

ing without overfeeding. Experiment with groundbait mixes until you get the right results and once you understand the basics you can indulge in some additives to make them more attractive. Never forget the ground rules! Those early mixes should only carry the free hookbait samples in small quantities to encourage interest in the hookbait.

PIKE BAITS

The choice of pike baits will depend on the methods you use and the waters you fish. You may need to use livebaits because you will be faced with preoccupied, fry-feeding pike or you may be faced with coloured water and find that deadbaits make a more viable option. Livebaits can be caught in advance or on the day, though you would be well advised to take along a supply of deadbaits as an alternative or as a back-up just in case no livebait is available.

You may not wish to use livebait at all but opt for deadbaits and lures for all your piking.

Either way, your choice of baits, particularly deadbaits, could not be greater. Walk into any good tackle dealer and you will usually find a freezer stocked to overflowing with a huge array of different baits. A few years ago, your choice would have been from herring, mackerel and sprats, then a new, revolutionary bait came on the scene – the smelt. You could not buy these from fishmongers as they had no commercial value. They originally came from power station outfalls on places like the River Thames and were a chance find whilst trying to find sprats. Their apparent mystical power has been attributed to their cucumber-type smell, but, in fact they were just different! On waters that had been heavily fished with mackerel, herrings and sprats, the introduction of a new bait with a different smell was almost guaranteed to be accepted as safe by the pike!

55

4 Barbel

The following chapters will cover the most popular running water species, namely barbel, chub, roach, dace, bream and pike. A book dedicated to a single species would allow a large, detailed introduction to the subject species, continue with chapters on location, feeding habits, weather and seasonal effects and finally, examine methods with which the angler might catch his quarry. As this book is about several different species, each chapter will be entitled by the species and there will be subheaded sections covering the individual aspects as outlined above. Space being at a premium, only useful information will be put forward and whilst other methods may well exist, those discussed will represent some of the most practical and efficient available. For those of you who wish to know more about any of the subject species there is a Further Reading list at the end of this book. Many of the older books listed will be available from your local library service; the remainder are current publications which you may wish to purchase for pleasure and future reference.

BARBEL

Barbel (*Barbus barbus*) inhabit the faster moving waters which run clear over bottoms

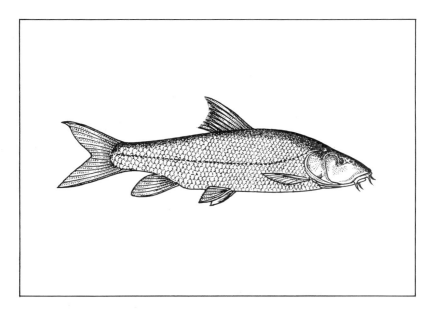

Fig 36   Barbel.

of gravel and between rich beds of weed, and weir pools where aeration generates high oxygen levels and food accumulates below the sill. The most notable rivers are the Hampshire Avon, Dorset Stour, the Thames, the Trent, the Great Ouse and the Middle Severn. Some of these are rivers that have been artificially created barbel fisheries and most of the stock comes from the River Thames. The Thames and the Trent, along with most Yorkshire rivers, were the natural homes of the barbel, these fish being related to pre ice-age ancestors of fish from the River Rhine and the River Elbe.

Many of the stockings were illegal and much frowned upon by most of the riparian owners who ran the fisheries for game purposes. Some river systems have barbel stocks infested with an Acanthocephan worm, *Pomphorhynchus laevis*. On game rivers like the Wye, where illicit stockings took place, it was feared that this parasite would affect the salmon stocks, but to date no serious repercussions have been felt. It is worth noting that the illegal movement of fish can have costly results, however (*see* Fig 36).

Identification

As a bottom feeder, the barbel is well suited to living in faster flows with its wedge shape. The eyes are very distinctive with their golden irises and the mouth is fleshy and underslung with two pairs of barbules – two on the upper lip and two at the back edge of the mouth. It is with these that the barbel locates and checks its food and our baits, before covering them with its large mouth.

Like most species, the barbel tends to take on a colour from the natural coloration of its environment. Most often it is greenish-brown or grey-green on its back and flanks with a much lighter, near white underbelly. The fins are in keeping with a fish with such a powerful body and a saw-edged spine is evident on the dorsal fin.

Spawning Habits

Spawning may take place as late as July and is dependent on a constant water temperature of 67°F. The other main requirement is clean gravel over which the barbel can congregate to lay and fertilise their eggs. On some rivers, extraction of water is leading to the silting of sections known to be barbel spawning grounds. The silt deposition is due to lack of flow.

Male fish carry white tubercules on their heads and flanks from just before to just after spawning, as do many other cyprinoids, notably bream. Hatching of fry takes approximately two weeks from fertilisation, but this depends on the temperature being maintained at 67°F. This is very infrequent in most river systems.

Growth Rate

Some river systems see the fry thrive, the Middle Severn being a prime example. With rivers heavily populated, growth is likely to be limited and large numbers of medium-sized fish will result. However, where spawning successes are poor and populations low, there is a chance of the fish to match the current record of fourteen pounds six ounces. In recent years, rivers like the Dorset Stour and the Wensum in Norfolk have regularly produced fish in excess of thirteen pounds.

LOCATION AND FEEDING HABITS

The barbel's love of fast-moving water, clear gravel and weed beds, is a recognisable characteristic when it comes to location. Taking

The wait begins with a white painted quiver tip silhouetted against the shadows on the far bank.

time to walk the stretch of river you intend fishing will help you locate either barbel themselves or at least the areas they are likely to frequent during the conditions that exist at the time of your visit and during times when the river will be affected by flood water. At times of flood when the river is at an increased level and heavily coloured, it will pay to know the whereabouts of slacks, eddies and obstacles like boulders, along the bottom, behind which a barbel may take refuge.

Whilst liking fast, turbulent and well-aerated water, barbel also like to take refuge in slack water as long as they can still be near to where food will pass and accumulate. To spend all its time in fast-moving water would prove very tiring for any species, including the barbel. However, the aerodynamic shape of its body allows it to spend more time stable in strong flows than most (see Fig 37).

Location

On rivers like the Hampshire Avon, where large beds of streamer weed grow, a good place to locate barbel is in and below the weed itself. If you are unable to spot any fish whilst walking along a stretch of river which has large beds of weed, interlaced with clear channels of swift flowing water, over a clear gravel bottom, try dropping in some free offerings of bait and watch while it is carried along by the current. In most cases you will notice a fish move out from the weed to intercept your bait samples. The barbel might only be prepared to leave the sanctuary and comfort of the weed bed for food that is on the move because this is how it receives most of it. It is worthwhile remembering this point when fishing in warm bright conditions and bites are slow on static baits.

Weir pools are another prime area in which

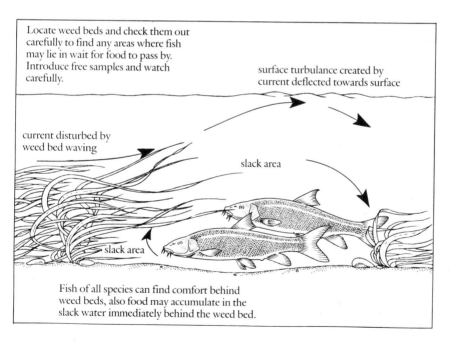

Fig 37   Barbel lying behind weed bed in slack water.

to look for barbel. They can find plenty of turbulent water here with a high oxygen level that
makes them comfortable and encourages
feeding, particularly in periods of warm
weather and low water levels. Also, there is
usually an area of almost still water along the
sill of a weir and it is here that food accumulates (*see* Fig 38).

Feeding Habits

When they are in the mood to feed more
intensely, then you will probably find barbel
moving in open water picking up food items
that are to be found on the gravel runs and
looking for small molluscs, shrimps, caddis
larvae and so on. Tempting the fish to take a
bait is much easier when they are in this sort of
mood – assuming that your swim is baited correctly!

Barbel tend to be shoal fish, particularly in
the small to medium-size range, although the
shoal could vary in size from three or four fish
to thirty or so. This depends on the river
system and stock levels. The biggest fish may
be loners who tend to stay out of contact with
these shoals. Their individual requirements for
food are likely to be greater than those of the
smaller fish. It is worth remembering this, and
any area where a big fish could lie and obtain
easy food supplies is an obvious place to
present your bait.

Holding Areas

Whilst the river is in flood conditions it would
be reasonable to expect the barbel to seek
sanctuary in slacks along the margins. This is
very often the case and fish may be taken from
their refuges behind obstacles such as bushes

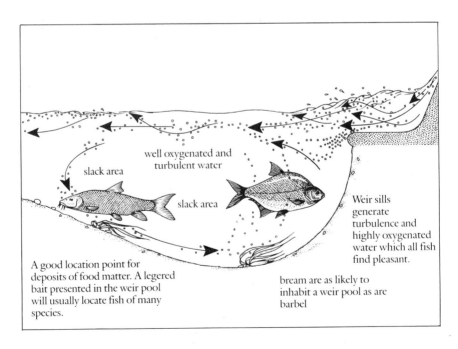

well oxygenated and
turbulent water

slack area

slack area

Weir sills
generate
turbulence and
highly oxygenated
water which all fish
find pleasant.

A good location point for
deposits of food matter. A legered
bait presented in the weir pool
will usually locate fish of many
species.

bream are as likely to
inhabit a weir pool as are
barbel

Fig 38   Fish lying in slack, aerated water below
weir sill.

and small trees submerged by high water. It is also likely that the fish will remain in mid-river and they will be seen topping in the fast surface boils. Many fish will be present on the bottom, taking advantage of the slack water created by boulders and obstacles on the river bed (*see* Fig 39).

Obstacles, boulders and variations in the bottom usually manifest themselves in the form of boiling, turbulent patches of water accompanied by bubbles. Weed beds may produce the same kind of phenomena, the turbulence will occur at varying distances downstream of the obstacles, according to the depth of water and the speed of flow at that point. Basically, the deeper the water and faster the flow, the further downstream the turbulence will show.

If you are to be a successful angler then you will have to work at locating your fish or likely swims and then spend time fishing them. Try baiting some of your chosen swims and then spend time watching through polaroids – you will learn a lot about your quarry and hopefully actually catch a lot more fish in the end.

WEATHER AND SEASONAL EFFECTS

Summer Fishing

Weather conditions will have a great deal to do with your success in catching your target species. The warm conditions of summer are all too readily taken for granted; though they can become a curse if they last too long and we suffer long dry spells with low water levels. The fish become lethargic and if it is really warm, the angler will be uncomfortable. Feeding is usually pretty vigorous during the warm summer conditions and early autumn. This is due to plenty of biological encouragement from the oxygen and warmth in the water. Bait attraction will be at its peak and flavours and oils will be more readily released from the bait and detected by the fish.

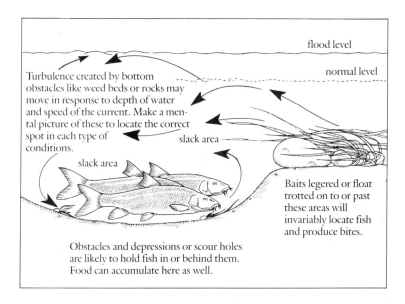

Turbulence created by bottom obstacles like weed beds or rocks may move in response to depth of water and speed of the current. Make a mental picture of these to locate the correct spot in each type of conditions.

flood level

normal level

slack area

slack area

Baits legered or float trotted on to or past these areas will invariably locate fish and produce bites.

Obstacles and depressions or scour holes are likely to hold fish in or behind them. Food can accumulate here as well.

Fig 39   Barbel in river bed depression.

A good Yorkshire Ouse barbel taken on luncheon meat.

(Above)   Quiver-tipping carefully perched on a floating reed bed.

(Below)   A roving approach to quiver-tipping with minimum of tackle.

BARBEL

Winter Fishing

The cooler, winter months from November to March witness a considerable change. Whilst it may be possible to catch barbel in the winter, and a few dedicated anglers do, it is only by choosing the optimum conditions that you can expect to succeed. The deciding factors will be the temperature and water levels. If water levels stay low due to extreme cold and there is no rain, the water temperature will fall close to freezing. At this low temperature the barbel's metabolism will indicate that feeding will not be necessary. In fact, the fish will slow down its activities almost to a state of hibernation, though it will remain alert and able to react to any crisis.

Winter Baits

In extremely cold conditions baits become almost unattractive in the scent and flavour sense – the cold water locks the oils and flavours into the bait, limiting their range. The addition of extra doses of flavouring to a softer, more soluble bait may help, but it will only be viable when water temperatures are upward of 35°F. The only hope will be a sustained warm spell accompanied by rain. The higher the water temperature, the greater your chance of catching fish – long live those warm wet winters!

METHODS

Having looked at locating barbel, their feeding habits and the effects of seasonal changes, we come to the methods with which you might catch the fish. You will need to combine all the aforementioned information and present your chosen bait, in the right conditions, at the right time, in the right place.

Some of the most successful methods are the simplest and there follows a selection of suggested approaches for barbel. The list is by no means exhaustive and other methods, most frequently adopted for other species, may work just as well – do not be afraid to give them a try.

The choice of a method for catching barbel will probably depend on two things – choice of bait and type of swim. You must get the presentation of the chosen bait correct for the prevailing conditions. For example, if the fish can be seen taking particles of food suspended in the current, it is more likely that you will succeed with a bait presented on the bottom.

Bait Dropper

A first choice bait for many barbel anglers will be luncheon meat, and you can see a terminal tackle set up for presenting luncheon meat in Fig 40. There are various ways of baiting with luncheon meat – you can dice your meat into half-inch cubes and offer them by throwing them upstream slightly to allow them to settle where you want them, or you can place them in a bait dropper and position them hard on the bottom of your chosen swim. Many anglers also use an attractor to help draw barbel into the swim and this is usually a bed of hemp, placed by using a bait dropper. The luncheon meat is then fished hard over the hemp, so accuracy in bait position is going to be very, very important.

Stringers

The rig shown in Fig 43 will help to get over some of the accuracy problems by carrying a supply of free offerings on the 'stringer' link. The link can be of PVA string or of a length of heavy line formed into a loop with a small piece of PVA pushed through the loop to hold the bait on to the nylon link. Both will depend on the PVA dissolving and water temperature

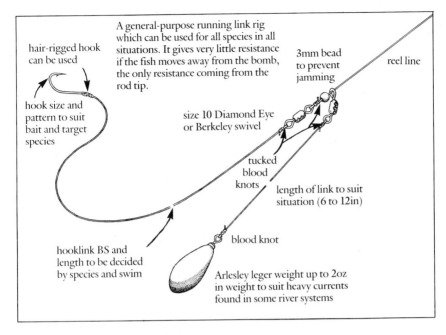

Fig 40   Running paternoster link.

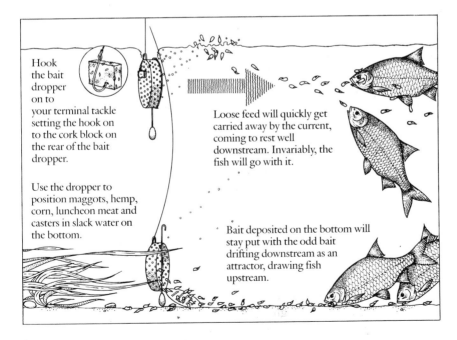

Fig 41   Bait dropper in use.

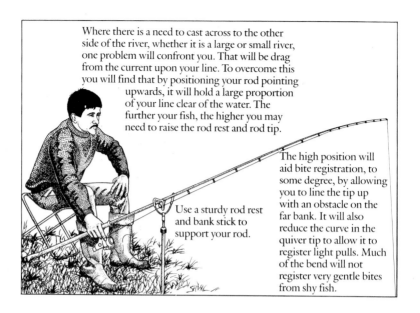

Where there is a need to cast across to the other side of the river, whether it is a large or small river, one problem will confront you. That will be drag from the current upon your line. To overcome this you will find that by positioning your rod pointing upwards, it will hold a large proportion of your line clear of the water. The further your fish, the higher you may need to raise the rod rest and rod tip.

Use a sturdy rod rest and bank stick to support your rod.

The high position will aid bite registration, to some degree, by allowing you to line the tip up with an obstacle on the far bank. It will also reduce the curve in the quiver tip to allow it to register light pulls. Much of the bend will not register very gentle bites from shy fish.

Fig 42   Bite indication with rod raised to reduce drag from current.

will play some part in this. It is a method that can be used well up until water temperatures drop considerably. Swim feeding with the dropper is a better alternative.

Swimfeeders

Swimfeeders are another means of getting baits directly into position, on the bottom, where the barbel can find them. Successive casts build up the quantity of maggots or hemp until a large amount have spread out around and downstream of the feeder position, drawing the barbel up to the swim. Shown in Figs 44 and 45 are various alterations to the Drennan feeder link and a rig layout. The feeders in Fig 45 are to allow the rig to be fished open-ended and they can be used with maggots or particles such as hemp and caster by using a fairly dry mix of groundbait to plug the feeders' open ends. Shown in Fig 46 is a common design of bait dropper and in Fig 41 you can see how it is employed in a fairly typical situation.

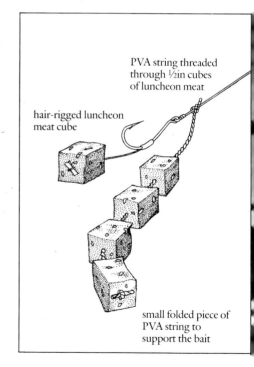

PVA string threaded through ½in cubes of luncheon meat

hair-rigged luncheon meat cube

small folded piece of PVA string to support the bait

Fig 43   Luncheon meat stringer link.

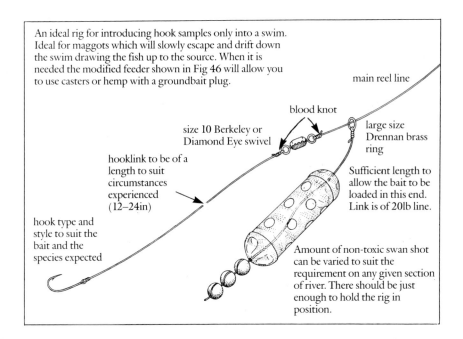

An ideal rig for introducing hook samples only into a swim. Ideal for maggots which will slowly escape and drift down the swim drawing the fish up to the source. When it is needed the modified feeder shown in Fig 46 will allow you to use casters or hemp with a groundbait plug.

main reel line

blood knot

size 10 Berkeley or Diamond Eye swivel

large size Drennan brass ring

hooklink to be of a length to suit circumstances experienced (12–24in)

Sufficient length to allow the bait to be loaded in this end. Link is of 20lb line.

hook type and style to suit the bait and the species expected

Amount of non-toxic swan shot can be varied to suit the requirement on any given section of river. There should be just enough to hold the rig in position.

Fig 44   Drennan feeder link rig.

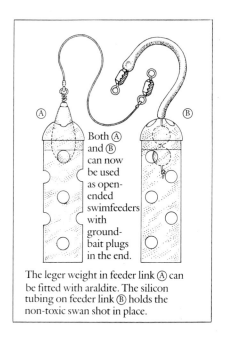

Ⓐ

Ⓑ

Both Ⓐ and Ⓑ can now be used as open-ended swimfeeders with ground-bait plugs in the end.

The leger weight in feeder link Ⓐ can be fitted with araldite. The silicon tubing on feeder link Ⓑ holds the non-toxic swan shot in place.

Fig 45   Modified Drennan feeder links.

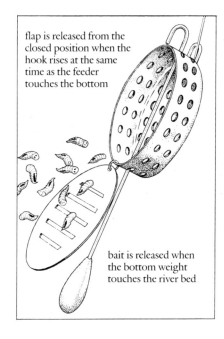

flap is released from the closed position when the hook rises at the same time as the feeder touches the bottom

bait is released when the bottom weight touches the river bed

Fig 46   Bait dropper.

5 Bream

In contrast to barbel, the bream (*Abramis brama*) is considered as a fish for slower-paced sections of a river system and its backwaters. Whilst this is, in the main, very true, bream can also be found in faster moving stretches of water and weir pools. They will be out of the main current and in areas that one may not have expected to find them. They usually fall to baits intended for chub and roach.

Large Catches

Of all the notable rivers, the Thames has a reputation for producing some heavy catches, but it must be the river systems of Ireland and the vast area of the Norfolk Broads that come to most anglers' minds, when phenomenal catches of bream are under discussion. Likewise the River Shannon and the River Inny. Most British rivers can produce reasonable hauls of bream – the Great Ouse, the Welland and the Witham are just a few. (*See* Fig 47.)

The bream is a bulky, deep bodied fish which can seem much larger at first sight than it actually is upon weighing! Fish in excess of seven pounds seem gigantic. Hooking and playing a large bream is a different story to

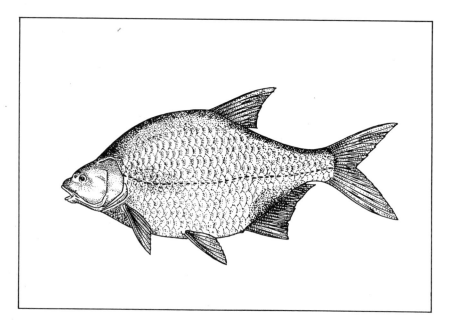

Fig 47   Bream.

looking one of the smaller examples. When playing a smallish bream, of say two or three pounds, in running water it may give the impression of being larger due to its ability to use its body size in the current. If you hook a really large fish, you may well think you have hooked a log, particularly if it kites across the current.

Identification

The bream is easily distinguished by its deep body shape and its large black fins (particularly the big forked tail and the very large anal fin). Dependent on age and environment, the general colour may vary from a golden-bronze young fish to a deep, dark bronze on older fish. A thick coating of mucus is evident on the fish's body. This might be one reason why a few anglers frown on the bream – it tends to cover everything it touches, landing net, keep net and clothing. However, it is fair to say that this mucus can be almost non-existent on bigger, more mature specimens. These bigger fish have a rather coarse, scaly texture which is far more acceptable. Whichever you catch, it is important to handle all bream with care. If you wipe off too much of this protective mucus the fish may become susceptible to disease.

Spawning Habits

Spawning usually takes place between May and July, and timing is dependent on the water temperature and geographic location (the further north the later it is likely to be). The indicator that bream are ready for, or are actually engaged in, spawning is the presence of white spawning tubercules on the head and flanks of the male. Spawning time allows a good sighting of just what fish are in a section of river. The shoals that form are very likely to be found in a slow backwater or side stream. A lot of rolling and splashing will be taking place. Most fish tend to reach spawning maturity at around five years but it depends on the environment.

Growth Rate

Fish within the range of three to five pounds are most frequently caught, but fish of a better weight do certainly exist. It is possible to turn up the odd individual fish of seven or eight pounds whilst roach, chub or barbel fishing. It may be that the bigger fish lead a more remote life than the smaller ones which are usually in large shoals. Double-figure fish do swim in our river systems but are caught too infrequently to make the majority of anglers bother to try and locate them. The River Chelmer in Essex held a large population of fish in excess of twelve pounds for a short period during the early 1970s. These were not indigenous fish but stock taken from Abberton Reservoir, near Colchester, and it was not long before they became significant by their absence. Whether they became cute enough to evade capture or died out is not clear, but their appearance was short.

One fish that appears in records compiled by Tate Regan in *Freshwater Fishes of the British Isles* is a bream that reportedly weighed seventeen pounds and came from the River Trent.

LOCATION AND FEEDING HABITS

There is only one sure way to locate bream and that is to spend time on the chosen stretch, having first ascertained that they should be there, early morning and at dusk being the best times. The areas to look at will be any backwaters and deep slow-moving stretches, but there is always the possibility that they will be located in shallower, faster-flowing water. Their presence will be fairly obvious, either by

A good haul of Hampshire Avon bream, taken on swimfeeder.

(Above)   Doug Allen and a beautiful weir pool bream.

(Below)   A fine example of a weir pool bream.

their continual topping and rolling activities prior to feeding, or large patches of bubbles coming off of the river bed, possibly heavily colouring the water.

Bottom Feeding

The feeding of bream has been likened to a flock of sheep grazing in a meadow – the shoal get their heads down and move along feeding. Bottom feeders, bream will be feeding on any food that is present there – small molluscs, larvae and so on, these being more evident and prolific in silty areas of the river bed.

WEATHER AND SEASONAL EFFECTS

Unlike some species that become less active in winter, bream will usually continue to be reasonably active although feeding is less intensive than in the summer months. Again, it is beneficial to take advantage of those warmer, wet periods of winter to have any real chance of success with river bream. Side streams and backwaters will be the places to search out the shoals, as they will seek to get away from the high water levels and fast currents of any winter floods.

METHODS

You will need to do some groundwork, firstly checking whether bream are actually present in the section of river you intend fishing and, secondly, doing some basic physical observation, possibly pin-pointing either a regular patrol route or holding area, dependent on the time of year. With this basic work done all that you need to do is select a method that will maximise the opportunity of catching.

Your choice of method and terminal tackle will depend on the circumstances prevailing at the time of your visit. If you are lucky enough to arrive at a time when bream are present and you suspect that they may actually be feeding, you will want to investigate the possibility of getting bites without introducing large amounts of groundbait, as you would if you were attempting to attract and hold a shoal of patrolling bream.

Paternoster

Having found bream feeding, the best rig for this situation would be that illustrated in Fig 52. It is a basic paternoster rig and whilst it will allow a sound presentation of your bait, it may need adjusting in its characteristics to obtain the optimum response. The hooklink may require lengthening or shortening to suit the way the bream are feeding. The ideal rod to use would be a quiver tip, with a tip to suit the general river conditions. Bait could be maggot or worm or even bread flake tipped with one of these as well.

Groundbaiting

A cast should be made into the feeding area to test the response (*see* Fig 48). If bites are forthcoming it may not be necessary to introduce any heavy amounts of groundbait, but it would be beneficial to commence a light feeding programme to hold the bream. Many anglers who intend fishing for bream commence, in many cases, by mixing and introducing large quantities of groundbait. If you were to do this in our hypothetical situation you would probably drive them up- or downstream. Very few fish would tolerate heavy amounts of feed being dropped on their heads. Introduction of your groundbait would be best made slightly upstream of the feeding area (in a loose, fairly dry mix form, allowing it to break up easily), to be carried downstream

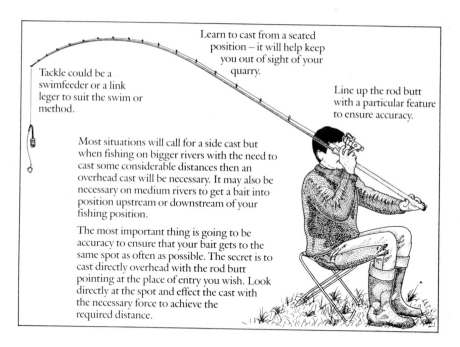

Learn to cast from a seated position – it will help keep you out of sight of your quarry.

Tackle could be a swimfeeder or a link leger to suit the swim or method.

Line up the rod butt with a particular feature to ensure accuracy.

Most situations will call for a side cast but when fishing on bigger rivers with the need to cast some considerable distances then an overhead cast will be necessary. It may also be necessary on medium rivers to get a bait into position upstream or downstream of your fishing position.

The most important thing is going to be accuracy to ensure that your bait gets to the same spot as often as possible. The secret is to cast directly overhead with the rod butt pointing at the place of entry you wish. Look directly at the spot and effect the cast with the necessary force to achieve the required distance.

Fig 48   Overhead casting from seated position.

Having made the cast in its first stage, the release of the line will be of importance in obtaining the maximum distance and accuracy. Only practice will get it all working correctly. Snatching on the cast will, if it occurs, empty the feeder if it is of the open-end type. The point of release will come at the moment the rod reaches its final point of travel with the tackle having come past the tip and beginning its forward travel.

Control of the cast is important to prevent the tackle going too far. If it is necessary to cast hard to get to the swim you wish, you can check the travel by feathering the line with your fingers. The other alternative is to use a side cast, if there is room, if you regularly over-cast.

Fig 49   Overhead casting.

to the feeding bream (*see* Fig 35).

However, you may arrive at your chosen swim and find no evidence of activity from the bream. In this case, you would be well advised to make an exploratory series of casts to check. It is always possible that fish are in residence and heavy groundbaiting will risk driving them away. If no bites or line bites occur, then feeding in your groundbait will be alright; but do not put it all in at once – build it up slowly, either by hand, bait dropper or swimfeeder.

Swimfeeders

If you choose swimfeeder, then the type you should choose will be found in Figs 50 and 51 – either an open-ended feeder or a cage feeder. The open end will require a dryish groundbait mix to form the two end plugs – maggots or hemp and casters in between. The cage feeder can be used in a similar way, but maggots are best left out of your groundbait, which should

be a fairly dry mix with the hemp and casters already mixed in. You then drop the feeder into the mix and squeeze an amount of groundbait into the feeder mesh. Then cast into the swim.

Hookbaits

If you have got the mix correct, shortly after casting and settling on the bottom, the groundbait plugs on the open-end feeder will dissolve, allowing the bait out. With the cage feeder, the feed will deposit itself on the bottom. If these are then fished in combination with hookbaits of either of the free offerings of bread, worms or cocktails, bites will eventually be forthcoming. If you are using bread flake on the hook then include some pinches of flake in your groundbait, both if you use it loose or with a feeder! Regular recasting will slowly build up the groundbait and any loose feed may carry downstream on the current, drawing fish up to your well-fed

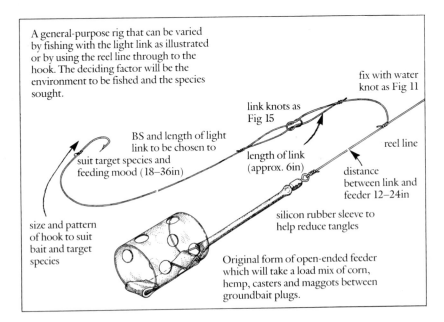

A general-purpose rig that can be varied by fishing with the light link as illustrated or by using the reel line through to the hook. The deciding factor will be the environment to be fished and the species sought.

fix with water knot as Fig 11

link knots as Fig 15

BS and length of light link to be chosen to suit target species and feeding mood (18–36in)

length of link (approx. 6in)

reel line

distance between link and feeder 12–24in

size and pattern of hook to suit bait and target species

silicon rubber sleeve to help reduce tangles

Original form of open-ended feeder which will take a load mix of corn, hemp, casters and maggots between groundbait plugs.

Fig 50   Open-end feeder fixed paternoster rig.

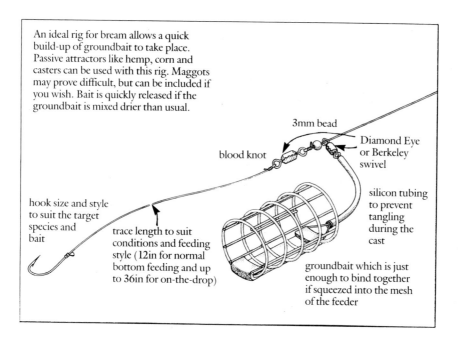

An ideal rig for bream allows a quick build-up of groundbait to take place. Passive attractors like hemp, corn and casters can be used with this rig. Maggots may prove difficult, but can be included if you wish. Bait is quickly released if the groundbait is mixed drier than usual.

3mm bead

Diamond Eye or Berkeley swivel

blood knot

silicon tubing to prevent tangling during the cast

hook size and style to suit the target species and bait

trace length to suit conditions and feeding style (12in for normal bottom feeding and up to 36in for on-the-drop)

groundbait which is just enough to bind together if squeezed into the mesh of the feeder

Fig 51   Cage feeder rig.

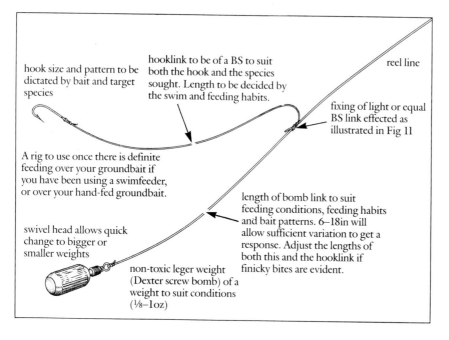

hooklink to be of a BS to suit both the hook and the species sought. Length to be decided by the swim and feeding habits.

reel line

hook size and pattern to be dictated by bait and target species

fixing of light or equal BS link effected as illustrated in Fig 11

A rig to use once there is definite feeding over your groundbait if you have been using a swimfeeder, or over your hand-fed groundbait.

length of bomb link to suit feeding conditions, feeding habits and bait patterns. 6–18in will allow sufficient variation to get a response. Adjust the lengths of both this and the hooklink if finicky bites are evident.

swivel head allows quick change to bigger or smaller weights

non-toxic leger weight (Dexter screw bomb) of a weight to suit conditions (⅛–1oz)

Fig 52   Fixed paternoster rig.

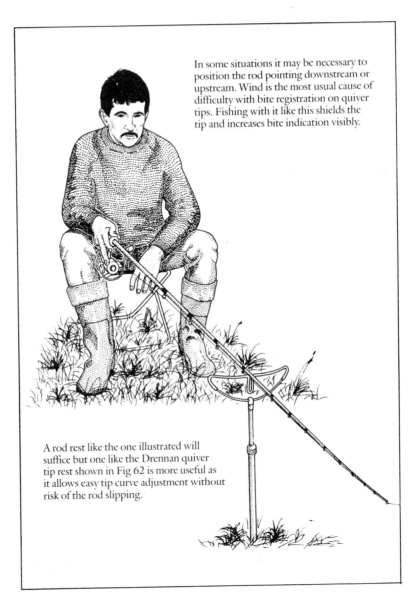

In some situations it may be necessary to position the rod pointing downstream or upstream. Wind is the most usual cause of difficulty with bite registration on quiver tips. Fishing with it like this shields the tip and increases bite indication visibly.

A rod rest like the one illustrated will suffice but one like the Drennan quiver tip rest shown in Fig 62 is more useful as it allows easy tip curve adjustment without risk of the rod slipping.

Fig 53   Quiver tip bite indication.

swim. Any patrolling fish should be able to locate it and sport should commence.

Alternative Methods

When bites do come, an important thing to remember is to try changing the hook and feeder link lengths to optimise the bite indication. It may also be beneficial to try using a fixed paternoster link (*see* Fig 52), to attach the feeder instead of the free-running rig or to use a block-end or feeder link with maggots only inside. It will depend on river conditions, the weather and time of year.

6 Chub

Of all the running water species, there can be little doubt that the chub (*Leuciscus cephalus*) is a 'target' fish for more anglers than any other. A totally omnivorous creature, it will eat anything that it considers as food, be it plant or animal, living or dead (although this will depend on the age of the fish). Smaller chub, in their early years, will take smaller food forms. Normal items like molluscs and larvae are supplemented by minnows and possibly crayfish in later years with the larger individuals taking eels also.

Spawning Habits

Spawning will take place between May and June but as with all species it will depend on the water temperature. The act of spawning may take place in side streams, tributaries or backwaters in shallow water, amongst plenty of weed. Eggs usually hatch within eight to ten days. The early months form a period of slow growth but this gathers momentum from the second year onwards. Males reach adult status at approximately four years and females at approximately five years of age.

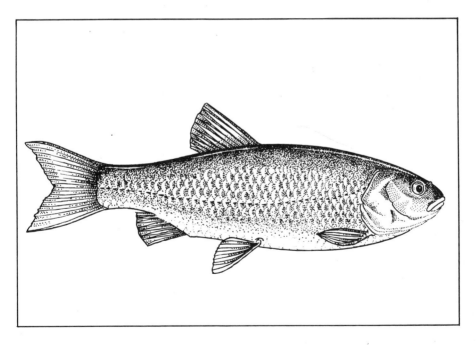

Fig 54   Chub.

CHUB

Identification

During its early years, the chub is very often mistaken for a dace but this is usually due to the angler's lack of experience and familiarity with either species. Coloration in mature fish may be deep olive green on the back, lightening down the flanks to a pale silvery white underbelly. The tail is thick with a very shallow 'V' and its dorsal is set well back towards the rear, in fact, over half-way back towards the tail. Probably the chub's most noticeable feature and one that identifies it quickly, both as it is netted and as it is spotted in the river feeding, are its large white lips surrounding its cavernous mouth. If this feature is remembered, very few people will fail to recognise the chub.

Not being a total bottom feeder, the chub

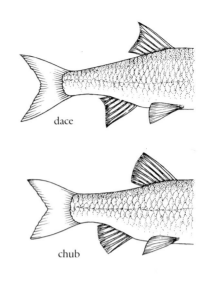

Fig 55 Chub and dace fin variations.

A classic small river raft, sure to hold fish.

78

A good haul of specimen River Wensum chub taken on the stick.

can be seen taking floating vegetable matter, leaves and seed pods along with the hatches of various insects at different times of the day. It is worth exploiting this mood when it occurs by offering surface baits.

Not all rivers contain chub and some that do, have been stocked. Rivers like Norfolk's River Wensum is an example. The chub here have been relocated from the River Wissey! To say that this has suited the chub would be an understatement as they have now heavily populated the whole river. Chub are persecuted by game fishery managers who fear that they eat small trout and salmon parr. Rivers like the Wye and the Upper Wissey are regularly electro-fished to remove all coarse fish stocks.

Growth Rate

This culling can have benefits, in that some of the larger fish escape capture. It can be these waters that produce the leviathan we all seek. With an approximate life span of twelve years, dependent on the environment, it is possible for a chub to grow to a double-figure weight. An old record was a ten-pound eight-ounce chub from the River Annan. This stood until 1969 when record fish lists were purged and this fish was deleted. The revised qualifying weight was set by the BRFC at seven pounds. A new record fish was submitted by Bill Warren in 1974 – seven pounds six ounces from the Hampshire Avon. This was eventually accepted and stands today.

A near record-breaking fish was also taken, in 1977, from the River Great Ouse, backwater. It weighed in at seven pounds four ounces and was caught by a local angler, Don Smith. The general feeling is the next record will come from a river like the Hampshire Avon or the Dorset Stour, but it could come from a small backwater on a river of minor significance.

LOCATION AND FEEDING HABITS

Ask any chub angler where to find chub and he will probably itemise over-hanging bushes and branches (particularly those with weed rafts), deep bends and any snaggy areas as well as many more individual locations that will be found by taking that much recommended walk along the river bank.

The importance of walking the entire stretch cannot be stressed enough, because although large shoals of chub may be present on bigger rivers like the Severn, the Ribble or the Trent, and it can pay to sit it out and build up a swim, populations can be low on smaller rivers. In many cases, only three or four fish are present in a given swim. Indeed, only one chub may be resident; though this one may exceed five pounds.

Holding Areas

A walk up or down the river will reveal many features which may hold one or more chub and if you take some mashed bread with you on your walk, you can bait your intended swims ready for later. You can fish them in sequence with any other swims you may find. The mashed bread will tell you exactly what the river's secrets are – the sort of under currents, where the slacks are, the undercut banks and where the current speeds up or slows down. All this information is very important if you are going to be successful, at first locating chub and ultimately catching them.

Cautious Fish

A very important point that should be remembered at all times is that the chub is a very shy and cautious fish. Every care should be taken in the visual and audible sense, in your approach to a swim, both for spotting and for

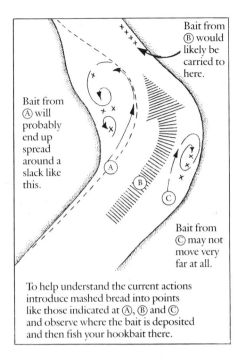

Bait from Ⓑ would likely be carried to here.

Bait from Ⓐ will probably end up spread around a slack like this.

Bait from Ⓒ may not move very far at all.

To help understand the current actions introduce mashed bread into points like those indicated at Ⓐ, Ⓑ and Ⓒ and observe where the bait is deposited and then fish your hookbait there.

Fig 56 Mashed bread swim feeding.

fishing. One heavy footfall, a dropped rod rest or too bold an approach can spook a shoal, making them suspicious or even driving them from the swim completely. Remember that a frightened fish is one least likely to want to feed or respond to even the most succulent bait!

Whilst chub like to frequent all the aforementioned snaggy holding areas, they also have a liking for steady-flowing water over clean gravel, particularly if there is some cover overhead. Side streams and backwaters, away from the strong flows of the main river are also areas to their liking, especially in flood conditions.

Fining Down

One of the most useful times to be on any river, in pursuit of chub, is immediately after a long period of rain when the river is dropping back to normal levels and it is fining down from all the muck and debris that all the extra water had brought with it. In conditions of flood, chub are wise enough to leave the main areas of flow and take refuge. When the river gets back to normal, they will feed quite freely on whatever bait is presented.

WEATHER AND SEASONAL EFFECTS

Summer sees more settled water levels on most rivers and these are usually low. At this time of year, the glides between weed beds are the best places to search out chub. Flow rates are going to be lower and generally more to the chub's liking in areas that, in the winter, will become intolerable.

Once winter sets in, a change in river conditions will usually mean a change in residence for the chub. They will take care to find comfort in times of strong currents. Fishing tends to slow but it is very rare not to be able to tempt any chub, even with ice on the river and snow on the banks.

Winter Fishing

The important thing to remember in the colder conditions of winter is to compensate for the slower metabolic rate of the fish by reducing the loose feed you put into the swims you will be fishing. Remember the roving fishing policy. It will reward you just as well if not better in the winter.

Baits

It is advisable to use an aromatic bait, to draw attention, because the natural flavouring may well become locked in during cold weather. It might be worth adding some flavour booster

A fine trio of chub taken on the float with a centre pin.

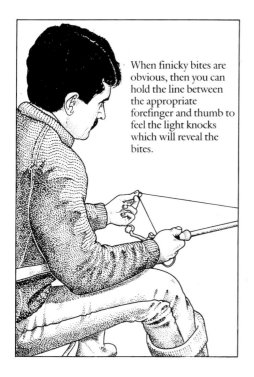

When finicky bites are obvious, then you can hold the line between the appropriate forefinger and thumb to feel the light knocks which will reveal the bites.

Fig 57   Touch legering.

that dissolves or washes off the bait. Add some flavouring to paste baits and groundbaits, particularly those with mashed bread. It will act as an attractor, both by scent and sight. Location of bait by smell is most important during times when a river is carrying a little colour.

You should also consider the texture of winter baits. Many baits will stiffen in cold water so make sure you allow for this when mounting them on the hook or make them softer. It is no good locating fish and getting bites that you cannot hook, particularly in the winter. Bite indication may be at its minimum in winter so be prepared to increase sensitivity, both here and with finicky fish, by holding the line between the butt ring and reel, between your forefinger and thumb. This is called 'touch legering', and it will help you 'feel' those gentle plucks.

METHODS

The method of fishing will, to some degree, be dictated by the river. Larger rivers lend themselves to every method in use, from the float, through all the various leger methods; smaller rivers may dictate a more narrow range, including float, light leger and free-line methods. The big problem is going to be which?

SWIMFEEDERS

Chub are, to their cost in the smaller sizes, fairly easy to tempt and catch, particularly the shoal fish found on larger rivers. In this instance you could use a swimfeeder and it should allow you to get a reasonable return from a day's fishing. Swimfeeder fishing with an open-ended feeder using maggots, casters or hemp held in by groundbait plugs will allow a fair amount of bait to be built up by regular re-casting until fish are forthcoming, each subsequent cast then topping up the bait. You may find that eventually you get bites as soon as or even before the swim feeder has landed on the bottom and emptied.

Fixed Paternoster

Terminal tackle can be laid out as detailed in Figs 50 or 58. You can also use a cage feeder or feeder link. Once the chub are feeding readily you may be able to dispense with the feeder altogether and fish a straight leger rig – either a running lead set up as shown in Fig 40 or a fixed paternoster as shown in Fig 52. There is one important fact to remember and that is the length of the tail from bomb to reel line and hook to bomb links. The need to vary this will be dictated by the feeding attitude of the chub. It might be necessary to increase the length or even shorten it to allow bold or finicky bites to register at the rod through your quiver tip.

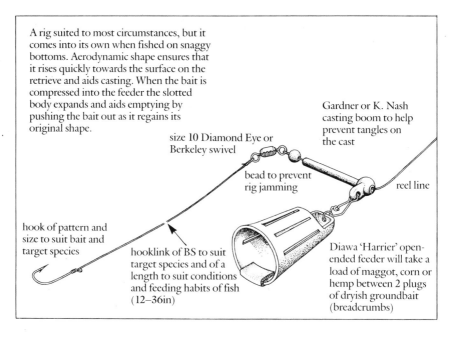

A rig suited to most circumstances, but it comes into its own when fished on snaggy bottoms. Aerodynamic shape ensures that it rises quickly towards the surface on the retrieve and aids casting. When the bait is compressed into the feeder the slotted body expands and aids emptying by pushing the bait out as it regains its original shape.

Gardner or K. Nash casting boom to help prevent tangles on the cast

size 10 Diamond Eye or Berkeley swivel

bead to prevent rig jamming

reel line

hook of pattern and size to suit bait and target species

hooklink of BS to suit target species and of a length to suit conditions and feeding habits of fish (12–36in)

Diawa 'Harrier' open-ended feeder will take a load of maggot, corn or hemp between 2 plugs of dryish groundbait (breadcrumbs)

Fig 58   Open-ended feeder (Harrier) rig.

Float Fishing

If you get the chance to offer your bait on the float, on a larger river, then stickfloat or even waggler float tactics will be worth using. A longish rod of about twelve or thirteen feet will be required for trotting a stickfloat through a selected run. You should team this with three- or four-pound BS main line, although it may be necessary to use a lighter hooklink. Start by fishing at least three-pound BS line straight through to the hook. You can see how to rig a stickfloat for various conditions in Fig 17 and Fig 18 illustrates the layouts for waggler fishing, rod and line requirements remaining the same.

Greased Line

When fishing with a stickfloat the line should be made to float – a sinking line cannot be used

at all. You can make sure that your line floats by greasing it with Mucilin or by using a line floatant spray like Leeda fly float which will require spraying on throughout your session. Mucilin is cheaper but you will need to dedicate a spool of line to it and clean the rings periodically, particularly if you change over to waggler fishing.

A floating line is very important in that it will allow the float and bait to travel along at the same pace as the loose feed and current. It also allows full control for correcting the path the line takes, particularly when more turbulent water is fished. This will pull the line away from the float and interfere with bait presentation. As it floats, the line can be picked up and 'mended' to run on the correct line once again causing only momentary interruption to an otherwise trouble-free trot.

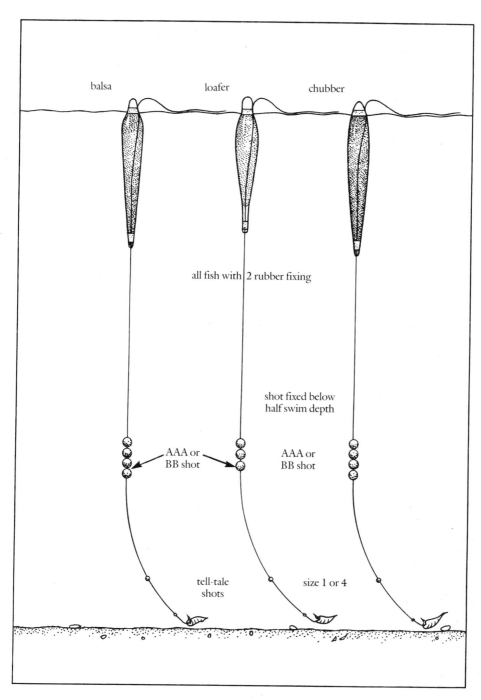

Fig 59 Assorted balsa floats and shotting patterns.

Waggler Fishing

The waggler can be used to slow down the rate of travel of the hookbait to suit feeding habits. Holding back with a stickfloat in fast currents, particularly where the surface water pushes along much faster than the rest, will raise the float and lift the bait off the bottom. The waggler, however, will be controlled more easily by sinking the line, and holding it back by fingering the line as it leaves the spool, allowing good presentation as the bait passes through the swim.

Shotting Patterns

Float size is important. Up to a point, choice will be purely personal, but the river conditions will dictate exactly what size should be used. Chub feeding habits will then suggest a shotting pattern – on the drop, fast sink to beat small fish or trailing bottom. Some basic patterns are shown in Figs 17 and 18. Heavier shotting capacity floats are to be preferred (5 or 6 BB or even AAs).

Upper Rivers

Moving away from the larger rivers and large shoals of small to medium-size chub, we move on to methods that will be better suited to the narrower, upper reaches of rivers where you are likely to be fishing for a better size of chub and maybe the specimen sized individual fish. Float tactics can still prove useful – the Avon float as shown in Fig 59, a balsa float or more directly a 'Chubber' which is designed to allow the presentation of bread flake or worm in the faster flows of the upper rivers. Shotting capacities around five or six AAs are ideal and will allow good presentation in most situations. Fig 60 shows some of the shotting patterns for the larger bodied floats.

Stalking chub on a small upper stretch of river.

An upper river chub.

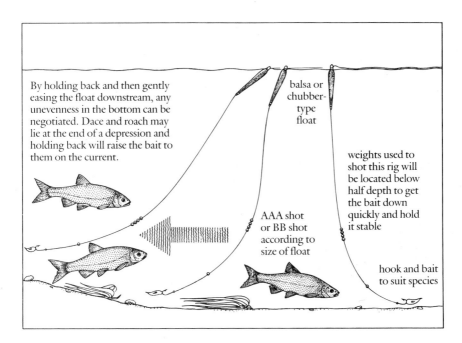

By holding back and then gently easing the float downstream, any unevenness in the bottom can be negotiated. Dace and roach may lie at the end of a depression and holding back will raise the bait to them on the current.

balsa or chubber-type float

weights used to shot this rig will be located below half depth to get the bait down quickly and hold it stable

AAA shot or BB shot according to size of float

hook and bait to suit species

Fig 60   Balsa-type floats in use.

Free-lining

Where the use of a float is ruled out by river conditions or because you intend fishing into dusk, then legering can be a beneficial method to switch to. Choice of bait will go some way towards influencing the choice of terminal tackle. You might choose bread flake, crust, cheese paste or luncheon meat. Then the remaining factors will be the type of water and the swim to be fished. Free-lining could be very useful, allowing you to work a bait through a slack, away from fast currents or even to allow it to be carried along by the current, both above and below the surface. Bread crust can be used to get a bait into a hotspot by weed rafts. The important thing here will be to pre-bait by putting in small free offerings to see if chub are taking surface baits. Only then should you put a hookbait through.

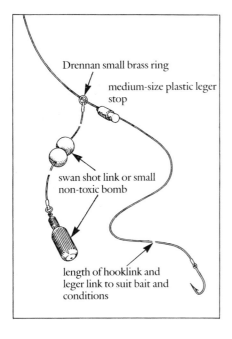

Fig 61   Drennan ring-link leger rig.

Link Leger

Usually, there will be a requirement for some means of holding down the bait in the current and for casting. Shown in Figs 61 and 72 are some basic terminal tackles for presenting bread flake, cheese paste and anchored crust.

Quiver Tip

Tackle for leger fishing in most of these situations will be well served by an eleven-foot quiver-tip rod, three- or four-pound BS reel line and hooks sized to suit the baits in use. If fishing near snags, five-pounds BS reel line may be a better choice.

The minimum amount of weight is preferred. In most situations, one or two non-toxic SSG shots (swan shots), on a light link leger will suffice, but this will depend on the swim – you must add weight until the tackle just holds! A bait dropper can be used to position a bed of hemp or casters to act as a fixed or mobile attractor, but as with all types of fishing, it can pay to put a hookbait into the swim before introducing any groundbait, the exception being when you walk the stretch and drop a handful of mashed bread into each swim you want to fish later, on your way back along the stretch. A chub or two may be resident and if your approach is cautious you may get a fish without any groundbait at all. If, after trying, no bites are forthcoming then you can try using a small amount of attractor. If necessary, keep up a light, slow but regular introduction of bait to entice fish up to the swim.

Roving Approach

Staying put in one swim may not be the ideal way to capitalise on chub and a roving approach will probably pay dividends. That way you can pick up one or two fish from each

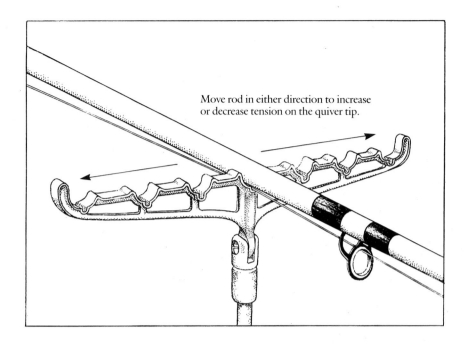

Move rod in either direction to increase or decrease tension on the quiver tip.

Fig 62   Drennan quiver rod rest.

swim. However, you should take a more static approach at dusk in a swim that has a good chance of producing some bigger fish.

Swimfeeder fishing can work on the bigger, wider stretches of river and any of the rigs shown in all the other chapters can be used. However, the loud entry of a feeder dropping into a swim can prove fatal on small rivers, spooking the fish. Remember that a frightened fish is not a feeding fish!

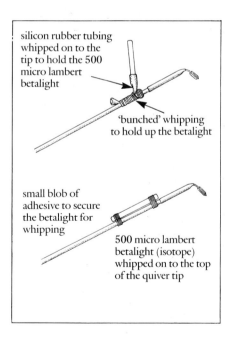

silicon rubber tubing whipped on to the tip to hold the 500 micro lambert betalight

'bunched' whipping to hold up the betalight

small blob of adhesive to secure the betalight for whipping

500 micro lambert betalight (isotope) whipped on to the top of the quiver tip

Fig 63   Quiver tips with betalight fitted.

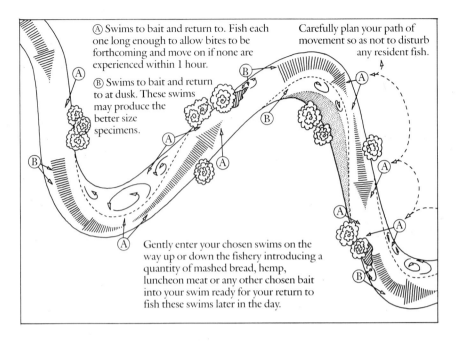

Ⓐ Swims to bait and return to. Fish each one long enough to allow bites to be forthcoming and move on if none are experienced within 1 hour.

Ⓑ Swims to bait and return to at dusk. These swims may produce the better size specimens.

Carefully plan your path of movement so as not to disturb any resident fish.

Gently enter your chosen swims on the way up or down the fishery introducing a quantity of mashed bread, hemp, luncheon meat or any other chosen bait into your swim ready for your return to fish these swims later in the day.

Fig 64   Roving and fixed swim locations.

Stealth and concealment are of paramount importance with all species on small- and medium-size rivers. It will be to your benefit once in a small swim to keep a low profile and avoid sitting above the skyline. To this end it would be advisable not to use a stool in tight swims on some stretches.

The handling mat you should carry will serve a dual purpose and give you a dry base to sit on.

angle of rod in rest will depend on conditions and flow

Use a rod rest of this type or the quiver rod rest illustrated in Fig 25.

Set a slight bend in the quiver tip to register drop-back bites.

Fig 65   Quiver tipping in a low position.

7 Dace

Identification

The dace (*Leuciscus leuciscus*) is a close relation of the chub (*Leuciscus cephalus*) (*see* Fig 66). The young of each particular species resemble each other to the degree that small chub can be mistaken for big dace. Close examination of the dorsal and anal fins will help distinguish one from the other (*see* Fig 55).

The dace is a fish for fast, turbulent, streamy runs over gravel, particularly in hot weather where dissolved oxygen will be at its highest level. It moves into deeper water in the colder months when water temperatures drop. Dace will be very active in warm weather, taking feed in the form of insects, both water-borne and off the surface. This type of activity will continue until the water temperatures drop to approximately 45°F. This seems to be the point where they become disinclined to feed. However, if there are any really deep sections on your river, you may find sport with some dace on these.

It is well worthwhile noting weather patterns and as soon as you suspect that water temperatures have risen several degrees, get on to your stretch of river to exploit what may prove to be a bumper feeding spell.

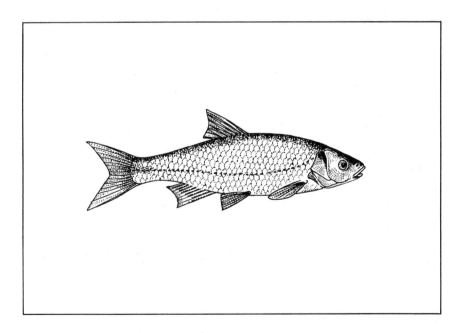

Fig 66   Dace.

Light Levels

Light levels seem to have a different influence on dace. Most species – chub, roach and barbel – tend to feed more actively during periods of weak and fading light, such as dawn and dusk, bites being minimal during daylight. By contrast, dace feed well during the brighter daylight hours and bites tail off at dusk.

Spawning Habits

Another contrary characteristic of the dace is its spawning. Most other species carry out spawning rites during daylight hours, sometimes carrying on into darkness. The dace carries out its spawning ritual at night. This spawning will take place in fast water over clean gravel and can occur any time between late February and May, weather conditions and water temperatures again having a direct influence. A mild winter and spring can see them finished by late February or early March.

Growth Rates

Fish in spawning condition will be evident by tubercules on the heads and gill covers of males. If there has just been a very mild winter this may be noticeable during the closing weeks of the season. Maturity is usually reached in two years with most adult fish living to an age of seven years. During those years adults may grow to any size between six ounces and the record weight of one pound four ounces and four drams taken from the Little Ouse at Thetford, Norfolk. The captor was a local angler, Mr J. L. Gasson and the fish was caught in February 1960. It is, therefore, a possibility that this could have been a fish carrying spawn. This particular fish is the present BRFC record holder. Bigger dace have been caught, up to a previous record weight of one pound eight ounces and five drams. It was caught, in September 1932, by Mr R. W. Humphrey from a Hampshire Avon tributary. This fish stood as a record until 1969 when new rules were set to establish that all record claims were bona fide.

Many rivers contain dace and many could easily hold a potential record but rivers like the River Thet, the River Wensum, the River Kennet, the River Wharfe and Hertfordshire's River Beane have shown they can produce record weight dace and could easily do so again. Suffolk farmer, Dennis Flack has many one-pound-plus fish to his credit from a local stretch of the Little Ouse, truly a river with potential.

LOCATION, FEEDING HABITS AND SEASONAL EFFECTS

Much of the information that can be written here has already been covered in the concomitant sections under other species. The dace is, basically, a lover of shallow, fast, gravelly sections of the river. These very often exist near bridges and if you look carefully over a road bridge you will probably spot dace.

During warmer periods shoals will be found in mid-water and on the surface, feeding on any surface feed in the form of insect hatches.

Winter Location

As the months roll by and temperatures drop or rain pushes the water levels up, dace will move into side streams, or into the deeper sections of river, to escape the effects of both cold and excess water. Location of summer swims will stand you in good stead for early, milder spells of cold weather. If there is deeper water close by, then this is where to look for dace if they have relocated. They will not move far.

Specimen dace may not be located in the

same quantities as their smaller brethren, but in shoals of perhaps six to ten fish. There may just be individual fish and these may frequent the deeper glides and slacks where chub reside. The key to location is observation and remembering the advice given in the preceding chapters. The main advantage of dace is their willingness to feed during daylight.

METHODS

Stick Float

Whilst it is possible to catch dace using leger tactics, the most pleasant method to use and probably the most consistent way to catch them is on the float. Stickfloat tactics are the most practical and some layouts using stickfloats can be seen in Fig 17. Dependent on the swim and the attitude of the dace, loose feeding a few maggots at regular intervals may help condition them ready for the first trot through with baited tackle.

Sufficient Control

Usual tackle of a twelve- or thirteen-foot float rod with two- or three-pound BS line, through a size 18, 16 or 14 hook will do for most situations. Floats will be of the stick style of your choice. The main thing is not to be tempted to go for too light a float; instead go for a fairly heavily shotted one to allow full control in what may be rather pacey conditions. Too light a load on the line may cause the bait to run through, well off bottom, and if the bait samples and dace are on the bottom, in winter, you will not find the rewards are forthcoming.

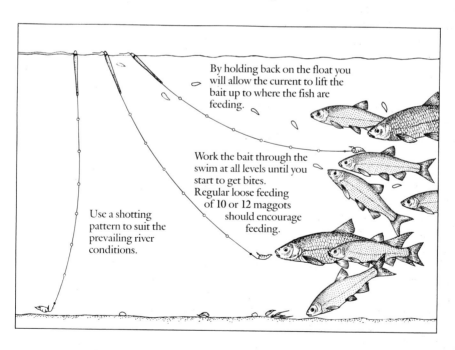

By holding back on the float you will allow the current to lift the bait up to where the fish are feeding.

Work the bait through the swim at all levels until you start to get bites.
Regular loose feeding of 10 or 12 maggots should encourage feeding.

Use a shotting pattern to suit the prevailing river conditions.

Fig 67   Holding back with stickfloat.

A good catch of specimen dace for Bruce Vaughan.

A good dace taken long trotting with the centre pin.

Long trotting for River Kennet dace.

Bait Choice

Casters can be used for dace but, with the type of lightning fast bites the dace usually give, it can prove frustrating reeling back empty caster shells. If you do decide to fish casters, sort out those that are at an intermediate stage between sinking and floating – these will be more buoyant and when fished on a fine wire caster hook, act similarly to the loose feed, particularly if you have dace feeding in mid-water. The hookbait acting slightly differently to the loose feed may put the dace off.

Feeder Link

For dace in deeper water, fishing maggot on swimfeeder rig, particularly in conjunction with a Drennan feeder link (Fig 44), may help when float fishing is impossible. Light link legered maggot can also be used, with maggots fed into the deeper swims with a bait dropper. In both cases bite indication would come from a sensitive quiver-tipped rod of the type discussed in the tackle section.

8 Roach

In stillwaters roach (*Rutilus rutilus*) have a natural ability to over-produce, resulting in a massive over-population if no predator species are present. This can result in stunting where small waters end up holding masses of two to four-inch fish. Whilst able to produce equally prolifically in river systems, up to 15,000 eggs per season are not blessed with a survival rate equal to that of their stillwater cousins.

Reasons for low roach populations could be poor conditions for spawning (which usually takes place between April and June, water temperatures being a deciding factor) or loss of fry due to weed cutting and subsequent flushing downstream in time of floods. Some rivers do, spasmodically, produce bumper stocks that survive into their second or third year, becoming mature and themselves able to spawn. This helps to boost stock levels.

Identification

Small roach can be slender looking fish and roach that live in bright, well-lit water can resemble small dace during their early years. Roach from deeper, darker waters are a fairly

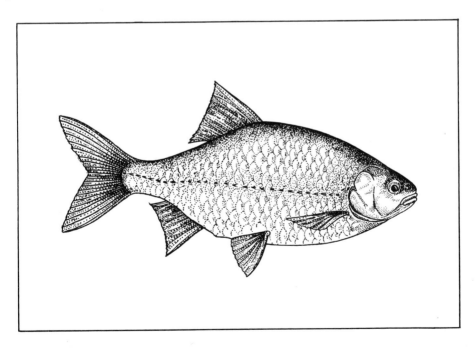

Fig 68   Roach.

deep green on their backs and flanks. Most notable of their features are the beautiful red pelvic and pectoral fins and the red irises of their eyes. Big roach can be very deep in the body, not at all resembling their small progeny.

Dependent on your target size, you may be easily pleased or disappointed. The one consolation of low fry survival is that the remaining stock of roach can grow into specimen sizes. Rivers like the Hampshire Avon, the Dorset Stour, Norfolk's River Wensum, and Suffolk's River Stour have, in recent years, produced three-pound-plus roach and it is the aim of many roach anglers to catch fish of this size or better. A two-pound roach is a more attainable target, though. The current record roach came from a Nottingham gravel pit. It was caught by Mr R. Jones and weighed in at four pounds one ounce.

Columnaris

Many of the fish in some of our river systems have suffered the ravages of columnaris. It had devastating effects on the roach in the River Wensum. Fish that survive this disease are usually identifiable by a reddening of the flanks and by displaced irregular scale patterns.

Spawning Habits

Spawning takes place in shallow water with plenty of vegetation on which the eggs and fry can establish themselves until ready to move. After a few days, they form into large fry shoals that can often be seen swimming close to the surface.

LOCATION AND FEEDING HABITS

Location of roach is usually not too difficult, particularly the smaller shoals of fish. If you

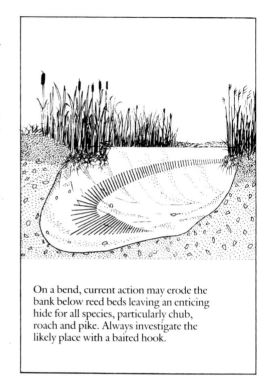

On a bend, current action may erode the bank below reed beds leaving an enticing hide for all species, particularly chub, roach and pike. Always investigate the likely place with a baited hook.

Fig 69   Undercut bend swim.

walk your stretch of river and study it carefully, at dawn and dusk, you will be able to spot the roach priming at the surface, and during daylight you may spot shoals under bridges or over gravel runs. Roach prefer slightly slower paced stretches on the bigger rivers, but they will tolerate the quicker flows of a stream.

Bigger roach are not such easy animals to spot – they like the seclusion of the deeper glides with some degree of cover in the form of reed beds or weeds. The deeper slacks and bends may produce in the right conditions. Swims that hold chub may also hold the odd big roach, so these are also places to put a bait.

The feeding habits of roach are pretty wide ranging. They take forms of larvae, crustaceans, worms and molluscs, whichever is most abundant in any particular stretch of the river.

Light Levels

Light levels seem to have a significant bearing on the feeding habits of roach. The lower the level of available light, either at dawn or dusk and, to some degree, as a result of water colour or cloud cover, the more likely they are to come on the feed. The latter two will give good sport all day.

Large roach tend to gather together in the evenings and having located a swim which they frequent or have taken up residence in, it is worth fishing it in the last hour before dusk, staying a couple of hours after dark or however long it takes to get a bite. These fish will quite often be seen topping well after dark.

WEATHER AND SEASONAL EFFECTS

Summer Fishing

Summer sees roach spread out over the entire length of the river, amongst the weed beds with their abundant insect life. Feeding in these conditions may be from the bottom to the surface, with the roach settling at a depth that is to their liking on any given day.

Winter Fishing

Fortunately, roach will feed in most temperatures. Winter flows and temperatures can even have a beneficial effect in that they can influence the fish to form tight shoals in the deeper runs and slacks which, if you can locate them, provide bumper catches. Flood water does not seem to have a detrimental effect on roach shoals providing the water is rain water with a reasonably warm temperature (around 40°F). However, cold snow water can be the kiss of death.

METHODS

Roach fishing probably invokes the thought of trotting a stickfloat down a classic glide in most anglers! There is probably a degree of Mr Crabtree in us all, handed down from father to son, and I suspect that this is at the root of it. In truth, the most effective method of extracting plenty of shoal roach from a swim is a float-fished bait. The stickfloat comes immediately to the fore but there are variations of this float each suited to different situations and there are also the waggler and various other specialised floats to deal with other river situations.

Throughout this and the other species sections you will find a variety of float tactics covered and illustrated. Those you will find here have become synonymous with river fishing and in particular roach fishing. Careful choice of the type of float and its shotting pattern are going to be of paramount importance if you are to succeed in catching consistently or in luring the larger specimen roach on a given stretch of river.

Choice of Float

Turbulent, fast water will require a totally different float, shot size and shotting pattern to a slower paced section of river. Figs 17, 18 and 59 illustrate some of the variations that may be suitable for different circumstances which may manifest themselves in the course of a day's roach fishing.

Stret Pegging

One of the least used methods that has some very practical benefits in the hunt for good roach is 'stret pegging' or 'laying on'. A common term used by stillwater roach anglers is that of 'laying on' but not so with river anglers. In Fig 70 you can see the basic layout with a waggler attached at both ends, as you

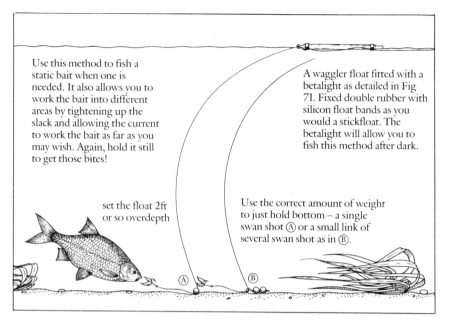

Use this method to fish a static bait when one is needed. It also allows you to work the bait into different areas by tightening up the slack and allowing the current to work the bait as far as you may wish. Again, hold it still to get those bites!

A waggler float fitted with a betalight as detailed in Fig 71. Fixed double rubber with silicon float bands as you would a stickfloat. The betalight will allow you to fish this method after dark.

set the float 2ft or so overdepth

Use the correct amount of weight to just hold bottom – a single swan shot Ⓐ or a small link of several swan shot as in Ⓑ.

Fig 70   Stret pegging with a waggler.

would fix a stickfloat. The rig is fished with all the weight, sufficient just to hold the bait and line down, in a fixed position. It looks very much like a lift method set-up. An AA or a swan shot, fixed at approximately six inches from the hook may require bolstering by two or three shots to hold the position in heavy flow. The key to success is to fish the set-up float rig three feet or so overdepth to allow the float to lay flat on the surface. In the stronger flowing rivers you may need more distance between the shot and float, but you will need to experiment to get it just right on your given river.

When bites come these will probably be positive cocking and sinking of the float without warning. Of all the methods, this one is probably the only effective method of night float fishing as it is a static float! Adding a five-hundred micro lambert betalight will allow high visibility. A modified Drennan insert crystal waggler would be ideal (*see* Fig 71).

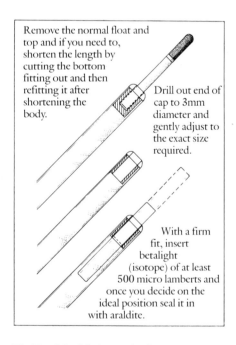

Remove the normal float and top and if you need to, shorten the length by cutting the bottom fitting out and then refitting it after shortening the body.

Drill out end of cap to 3mm diameter and gently adjust to the exact size required.

With a firm fit, insert betalight (isotope) of at least 500 micro lamberts and once you decide on the ideal position seal it in with araldite.

Fig 71   Modified waggler float.

Stret pegging is practical in more ways than one. Having made the initial cast and aligned the float immediately downstream of your rod tip and had no bite indication, you can work the bait downstream by lifting the line and tightening everything up, thereby dislodging the shot and letting the current carry it and the bait a yard or two further downstream. This will allow you to search the swim progressively, holding the bait static for as long as you feel is necessary to tempt a bite. Stret pegging is not a roach-only method and it can be used as an alternative for chub, barbel and bream.

Loose Feeding

To obtain the best results from static, slow-moving bait presentation you will need to feed accurately every time you introduce your loose feed. If you are working to a tight line and allowing the current to guide your float and tackle you must feed this self-same line exactly to ensure that you do not pull the fish away. It is surprising how many anglers fail to catch consistently by feeding the wrong line, actually driving the fish away from the hook-bait. Set a line and stick with it, feeding five to ten maggots or casters every trot through, be it fast or slow.

Static Baits

On some days, the only bait a roach will take is a static or as near stationary as possible or at least a very slow-moving bait, particularly in the depths of winter. It is worth bearing all of this in mind when setting out to catch them. You could adopt waggler tactics with the bait fished well overdepth as in Fig 18 and literally inched through the swim. You must make every effort to work a bait through the swim at each pace and depth until you locate roach and get some bites.

Undercut Bank

With some swims, particularly the deep bends where the flow drives to the opposite bank, as shown in Fig 69, and there are reeds and so on growing out over the top of the undercut bank, it will be almost, if not absolutely, impossible to present a bait correctly with a float so you will need to resort to a leger method to gain the optimum result if roach are present in the particular swim.

Link Leger

A light link leger, similar to that in Figs 72 and 61 will be sufficient. Bait may be bread flake, bread paste, crust, maggot or caster, the latter two being fished on a lighter hooklink, possibly with a smaller hook size to match.

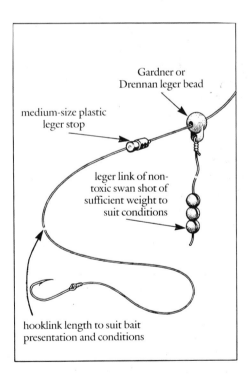

Fig 72   Link leger with leger bead.

Andy Jubb and a fine weir pool roach.

Long trotting on the River Waveney.

A fine feeder-caught roach.

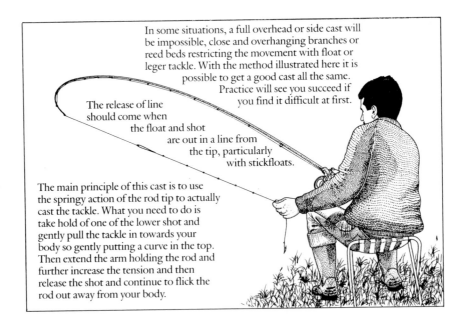

In some situations, a full overhead or side cast will be impossible, close and overhanging branches or reed beds restricting the movement with float or leger tackle. With the method illustrated here it is possible to get a good cast all the same. Practice will see you succeed if you find it difficult at first.

The release of line should come when the float and shot are out in a line from the tip, particularly with stickfloats.

The main principle of this cast is to use the springy action of the rod tip to actually cast the tackle. What you need to do is take hold of one of the lower shot and gently pull the tackle in towards your body so gently putting a curve in the top. Then extend the arm holding the rod and further increase the tension and then release the shot and continue to flick the rod out away from your body.

Fig 73   Casting with a stickfloat.

Pre-baiting

If the bend appears to be similar to the one illustrated in Fig 58 then there will be some slack water in the deep section under the bank and it is here that you should place your bait. If, as recommended, you are walking along the river pre-baiting likely swims, then use mashed bread groundbait to give you some guidance as to what the water is doing. Is there an eddy or static water? Watch what the mashed bread does, and offer your bait in such a way that it will end up where the ground bait does.

9 Pike

Identification

The pike (*Esox lucius*) (Fig 74) is immediately recognisable unlike some of the Cyprinoid species. It has a long streamlined body with a large tail and rearward-set anal and dorsal fins which allow strong, rapid acceleration to catch its prey. Its large, tooth-filled mouth is designed to deal easily with live, very slippery prey and throw fear into those who catch a pike by mistake. The body has a mottled effect. There are deep greens and browns (dependent on environment) fading down the flanks to a creamy, almost white, underbelly, which supplies the fish with camouflage. It can conceal itself from its prey in weed beds until able to strike effectively. The mottling effect alters throughout the early years and bar markings change to more broken patches covering the whole body. These markings become very distinctive in later years and along with the similar style markings on the fins, allow accurate identification of individual fish – as accurate as human finger prints, in point of fact.

The eyes, high on the head, are the reason why the pike is particularly successful as a pred-

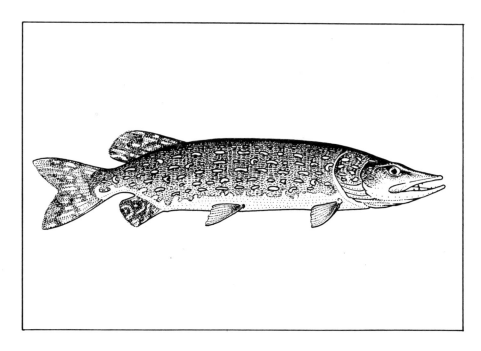

Fig 74   Pike.

Dave Wilson plays a relief channel pike.

ator. The position of the eyes gives the pike binocular-type vision forwards so that it can judge exactly the distance to its prey when striking to kill. They also allow good upward vision and it is this that you, as the angler, should note when presenting bait. If the pike is lying stationary on the bottom amongst weed, a bait passing over its head is more likely to be investigated than a static bait lying on the bottom some distance away.

Sense of Smell

The pike's olfactory organs are sited just forward of the eyes. This allows any scent in the water from a food source to pass over them whilst the pike is moving forward or lying in the current. It is important to note that pike are very capable of locating deadbaits in coloured water. Livebaits may be located by vibration through the lateral line, but smells travel further in the water giving the pike a greater location range.

Growth Rate

The majority of recaptures of known fish seem to indicate that annual increases in weight vary between one and three pounds but more usually one and a half to two pounds. This does not take into account the spawning period when a further two to five pounds of weight might be carried dependent on the fish's normal size. The female of the species is the bigger, the male fish rarely, if ever, exceeds ten pounds in weight and is often caught from seven to nine pounds when matured. No noticeable year to year increase in weight has been noted in known male fish recaptures.

Spawning Habits

Spawning usually takes place between March and April each year. Once the temperature of the water starts to rise above 40°F the urge to get spawning sees pike congregating on their regular spawning sites. The males usually appear first in quantity, followed by the females. Some phenomenal catches have taken place on water when anglers have located, usually by chance, just such a congregation of pike.

Knowing just a little about the pike may help you, but if you would like to learn more, then the Further Reading list at the back of this book will be of some assistance.

LOCATION AND FEEDING HABITS

Depths and Contours

There is no instant way to locate pike, large or small, on any river of any size. The smaller rivers might seem easier than the larger, but all things are relative! What is needed is some understanding and knowledge of the rivers you intend fishing. This cannot be gained without some effort on your part. Only after you have acquired the basic information of depths, contours, fish stocks and types and weed beds can you really expect to be able to decide which area or swim will produce what you are seeking.

Changes in Behaviour

During the course of a season, there are some distinct changes in pike behaviour. From the beginning of the season in June and throughout each of the summer months of July, August, and September, there is very little visible activity from the pike, mainly due to the fact that they are more evenly spread at this time of year and tend to use the cover afforded by generous weed growth to ambush their prey as they swim by. This might be why summer catches are greater for the lure angler who exploits the opportunity of clear water, weed bed fishing.

Autumn Fishing

From the end of September, there is a tendency for pike activity to become more visible and from early October this builds up to a peak as the fish feel the onset of winter and feed ravenously. This activity is usually coincidental with weed beds dying and fry shoals, reaching their larger individual sizes, becoming very visible with fry scattering at the surface. Occasional swirls and boils are visible as pike attack near the surface.

Winter Fishing

As November arrives so do the first hard frosts and water temperatures fall, driving the fry and food fish into deeper water followed closely by the pike. This is when all that research into contours, depths, etc. will pay dividends, because you will know where the fish may have gone and will be able to identify which swims are likely to offer the best opportunities of relocating them.

Seasonal Hotspot

It is possible that pressure from angling will drive pike into new areas. When the fry shoals become confined in one area, so do the pike and this can generate a seasonal hotspot which may produce some very large catches of good pike for the knowledgeable angler.

Roach Shoal Locations

During the colder periods of winter it is unlikely that most rivers will be carrying flood or excess water. They are more likely to be low and clear with some lower reaches low in flow,

icing over during the hours of darkness. Even some of the upper reaches will freeze if they are not fast moving. This generally makes for difficult fishing, but when the temperatures do rise the rivers quickly open up and fishing can be good again immediately after a short thaw commences, (one which would have had no effect on your stillwater).

Ideally, you should be on the river both early and late to locate the roach and dace shoals, if they exist. Where you find these, are the areas you should concentrate on fishing. During the winter months on tidal rivers when there are periods of high tides, the food fish will be pushed up into areas of river not too heavily affected by salt water. In times of flood there is still a chance of getting amongst the pike, as the shoals of food fish will seek refuge from the strong current, and will be accompanied by numbers of pike. If you have taken time to research your favoured stretch of river you will be able to predict which areas will hold a head of pike in a feeding mood. There could be a deeper stretch of river bed where a slack exists below the main force of flood water, a slack area or back eddy on a bend where the main stream of current hits the opposite bank. The mouth of a stream or drainage ditch which is flooded may provide a refuge, as will boatyards, etc. and dykes. You will know what exists on your river if you have taken the trouble to search. Try them all until you locate your quarry.

WEATHER AND SEASONAL EFFECTS

The whole subject of the effects of weather upon a water is related to the season. Traditionally, the seasons for pike fishing have been autumn and winter, commencing in October and ending in mid-March. Within that period there are likely to be changes in the weather

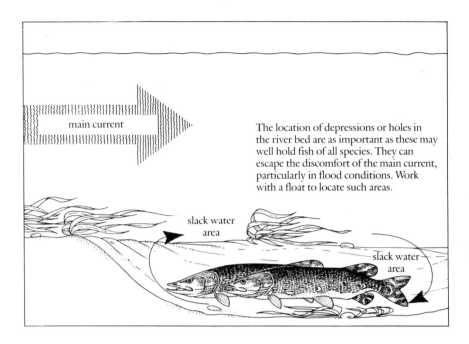

The location of depressions or holes in the river bed are as important as these may well hold fish of all species. They can escape the discomfort of the main current, particularly in flood conditions. Work with a float to locate such areas.

main current

slack water area

slack water area

Fig 75   Pike river bed hollow.

from warm, mild, damp conditions in October and November to extremely cold, frosty, snowy conditions in December, January and February. Then it will turn milder again with the close of February and beginning of March.

Barometric Pressure

Mild, damp and windy weather associated with a low barometric pressure will have differing effects on waters only a few miles apart or even hundreds of miles apart. During these conditions pike may become lethargic, and not wishing to feed on a moving bait they will be more likely to seek out a static deadbait. High barometric pressure which may bring cold frosty weather, clear skies and windless conditions, will see the pike more likely to seek out livebaits, but this may vary from water to water.

You will probably be asking how you can use knowledge of barometric pressure to your advantage. The important thing to do is to note the type of prevailing fronts over the country and to establish if there is a persistent high or low over your area. That way, you will be able to predict the sort of response you will get from the pike in your waters to livebaits, lures or deadbaits. A long-term low will give wind and rain and subsequently coloured water conditions and deadbaits will usually outfish livebaits as the pike may be feeding by smell.

A long-term high pressure front will lead to clear water conditions due to frosts and low water temperatures which will reduce algal colorations making livebaits and lures a more viable proposition than deadbaits. Of course, you might find that the reverse is true and that brings us back to where this chapter started. Above all, familiarity with a water will help you choose where to fish in given situations. There is no substitute for experience gained on the bank.

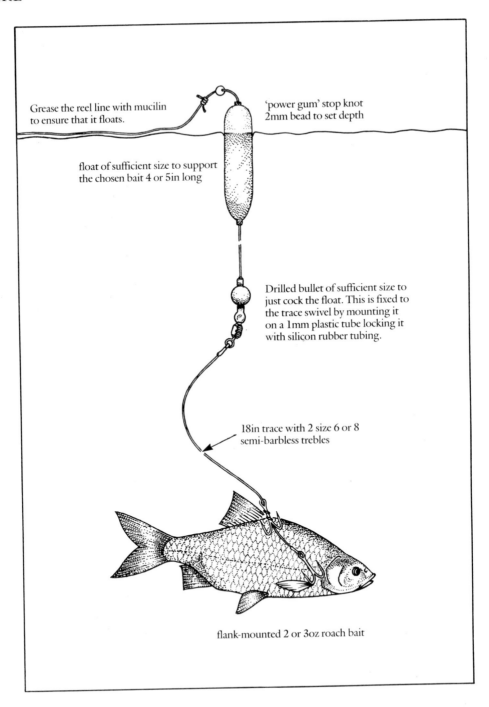

Grease the reel line with mucilin
to ensure that it floats.

'power gum' stop knot
2mm bead to set depth

float of sufficient size to support
the chosen bait 4 or 5in long

Drilled bullet of sufficient size to
just cock the float. This is fixed to
the trace swivel by mounting it
on a 1mm plastic tube locking it
with silicon rubber tubing.

18in trace with 2 size 6 or 8
semi-barbless trebles

flank-mounted 2 or 3oz roach bait

Fig 76   Free-roving livebait rig.

METHODS

Trotting

None of the methods discussed in previous chapters are suitable for catching pike in running water. Only one is vaguely similar and that is trotting a bait through a swim. We have seen this with stickfloat and waggler float tackle. Trotting a bait for pike is similar but some variations in tackle will be necessary. Of all the methods for catching pike, it is probably the most effective.

In Fig 76 you will see a free-roving rig that would suit many situations. To be at its most effective it should be used in conjunction with a livebait. In no way is it obligatory to fish with livebaits but if you wish to achieve any real success then you will need to consider that option. If you are not prepared for using livebait then try deadbait, roach or other dead coarse fish, or if these are not available then try sea baits like small horse mackerel, mullet or any sea fish that are durable. Herring and sprats are usually too soft to withstand the pressure of flowing water.

Free-Roving Bait

When using the illustrated rig, there are two methods of mounting the bait – in front of the dorsal and behind the pectoral as in Fig 77 or lip-hooked with the end treble in front of the pelvic fins. The flank-mounted bait retains the bait position whilst it is moving on the trot, but becomes handicapped when held back to cause the bait to rise in the current. Lip-hooking is preferable in most situations with this method as it will allow you to work the bait and create an attractive, enticing meal for our quarry. Fig 78 shows how you can use the current and float rig to achieve this. You can

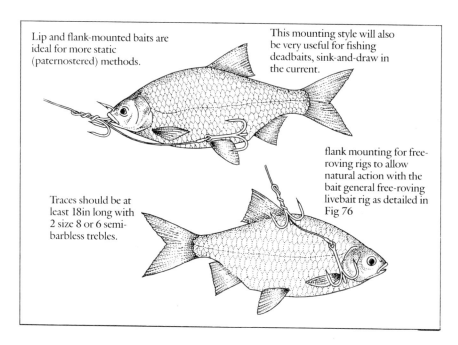

Lip and flank-mounted baits are ideal for more static (paternostered) methods.

This mounting style will also be very useful for fishing deadbaits, sink-and-draw in the current.

flank mounting for free-roving rigs to allow natural action with the bait general free-roving livebait rig as detailed in Fig 76

Traces should be at least 18in long with 2 size 8 or 6 semi-barbless trebles.

Fig 77   Livebait hooking position.

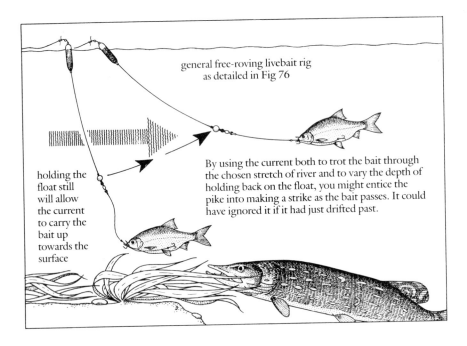

general free-roving livebait rig
as detailed in Fig 76

By using the current both to trot the bait through
the chosen stretch of river and to vary the depth of
holding back on the float, you might entice the
pike into making a strike as the bait passes. It could
have ignored it if it had just drifted past.

holding the
float still
will allow
the current
to carry the
bait up
towards the
surface

Fig 78   Trotting livebait.

work the bait through at variable depths covering all the likely holding areas by snags, slacks and side streams, etc.

Whilst there are obvious advantages to having a natural free-roving bait in a natural environment, there are times when pike, like roach want a static bait. This may be when there is a heavy flow to the river and it would cause the fish great discomfort to take a bait in fast water, so it settles for taking bait that does not require too much effort.

Paternoster

Swims that would suit the paternoster are the slack water on bends, deep undercut banks and areas by side streams that enter the main river. When a static bait is required, the method to use will likely be a paternostered livebait, or, if you feel the need, a deadbait. Fig 79 shows how to rig a paternoster. It could be a surface-fished float or a sunken-float paternoster.

Where the current is turbulent then it is quite likely that the float will sink anyway! With a sunken-float rig there is no need to be 100 per cent positive of swim depth, unless it is a fairly shallow swim, when it may be better to locate a deeper one than try to fish it.

Bite Indication

The ideal swim will be deep and undercut. Once you have placed a bait, the important thing is to ensure that there is tension between float and rod tip and that you use a drop-arm indicator as shown in Fig 80. Quite often, the first indication that your bait has been taken will be a drop back of the indicator. This is the pike taking the bait upstream. Sometimes this will be followed by a full-blooded run. Often the first stage goes unheeded, because there is no means of registering the slack line. The resulting hooked fish may, in fact, be deeply hooked because it was able to turn and

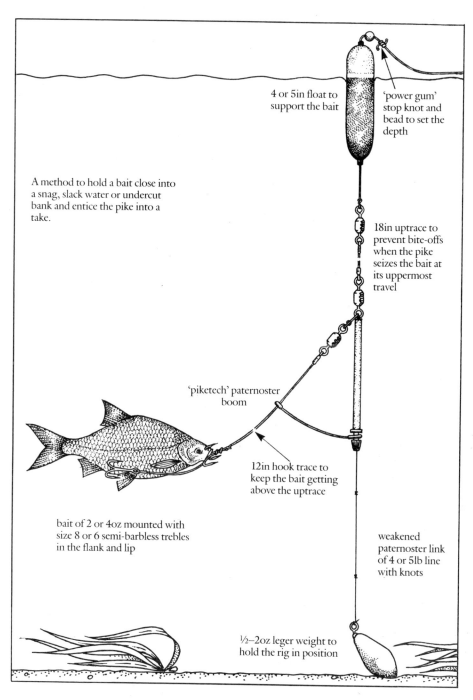

4 or 5in float to
support the bait

'power gum'
stop knot and
bead to set the
depth

A method to hold a bait close into
a snag, slack water or undercut
bank and entice the pike into a
take.

18in uptrace to
prevent bite-offs
when the pike
seizes the bait at
its uppermost
travel

'piketech' paternoster
boom

12in hook trace to
keep the bait getting
above the uptrace

bait of 2 or 4oz mounted with
size 8 or 6 semi-barbless trebles
in the flank and lip

weakened
paternoster link
of 4 or 5lb line
with knots

½–2oz leger weight to
hold the rig in position

Fig 79   Paternostered livebait.

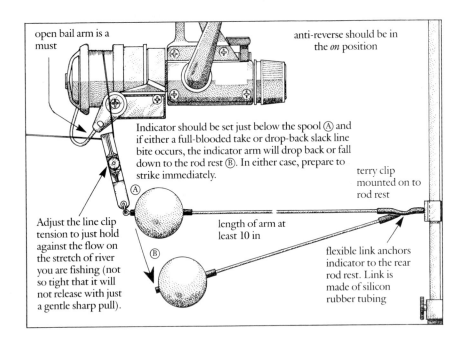

open bail arm is a must

anti-reverse should be in the *on* position

Indicator should be set just below the spool Ⓐ and if either a full-blooded take or drop-back slack line bite occurs, the indicator arm will drop back or fall down to the rod rest Ⓑ. In either case, prepare to strike immediately.

terry clip mounted on to rod rest

Ⓐ

Adjust the line clip tension to just hold against the flow on the stretch of river you are fishing (not so tight that it will not release with just a gentle sharp pull).

length of arm at least 10 in

Ⓑ

flexible link anchors indicator to the rear rod rest. Link is made of silicon rubber tubing

Fig 80   Drop-off bite indicator.

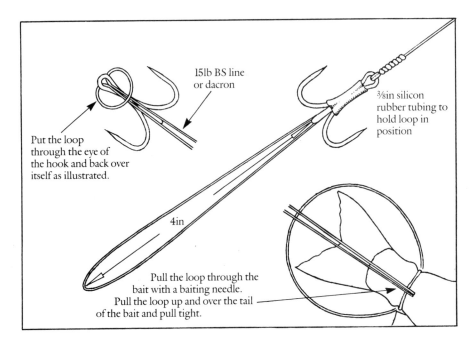

15lb BS line or dacron

⅜in silicon rubber tubing to hold loop in position

Put the loop through the eye of the hook and back over itself as illustrated.

4in

Pull the loop through the bait with a baiting needle. Pull the loop up and over the tail of the bait and pull tight.

Fig 81   Hair-rigged deadbait.

Mike Woods with a nice pike on trotting livebait.

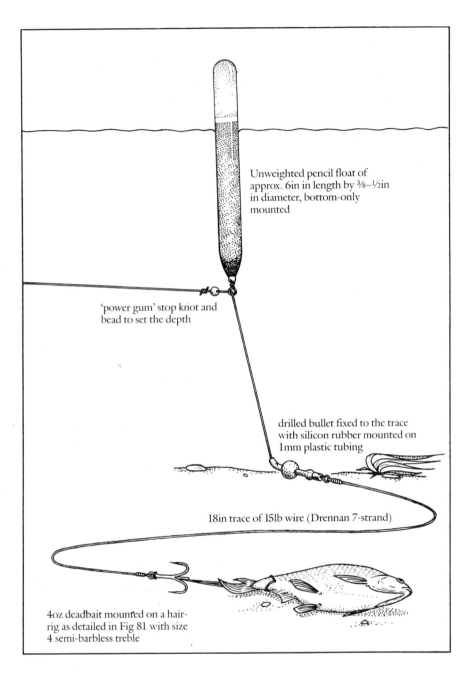

Fig 82   Deadbait float rig.

swallow the bait on the spot before moving off again! Audible versions of this type of indicator are available or the drop-arm indicator can be used in conjunction with an Optonic indicator.

10 Handling and Fish Care

Having illustrated the need for an understanding of species, the tackle, location and feeding habits and method, the next stage of the game is landing, handling and eventually releasing an unharmed fish.

In a way, this chapter of a book ought to be at the beginning, because fish care and handling should be very much a part of the initial planning of any fishing trip. Your choice of method and its hooking style are as important as that of landing net and weigh sling. Unhooking materials need consideration, as will your means of retaining your catches should you choose or need to for any reason. The most likely reason will be the wish to photograph a good catch or individual fish.

Landing-net

It may seem obvious to say that a good-quality landing-net is important, but some anglers go ill-equipped to land fish in certain situations. Having the wrong handle or the wrong mesh can all contribute to injuring or losing a fish or fishes.

Too short a handle may mean that you are unable to reach over weed or down steep banks. An extending telescopic handle may not seem macho to some anglers, but it can pay to carry one of at least three sections building up to approximately three yards. If you wish to use it shorter take off one of the sections, but do not get caught short!

Landing-nets need a little thought – a fairly open, micro-mesh pan net is superb, the bigger the diameter, the better (eighteen or twenty inches being the ideal for all species). A triangular net with 36-inch arms may be necessary for bigger pike. The round shaped net allows you to have a better chance of getting the fish in from any angle, a triangular net has limited angles of access. The openness of the mesh is important to allow the water to pass through when holding it out in the current. When you are netting your fish, do it with the net downstream of the hooked fish. This will allow the current to bring the fish to the net. Never lift the fish over marginal snags, etc. on the line, unless it is a small roach or dace, as you will risk losing your fish or even injuring it.

Handling Mats

Once you have your catch netted, unhook it swiftly in the landing net, supported on your knees and either return it or retain it. If it is a good fish take it to a soft grassy area for unhooking. If necessary, lay out a handling pad, like the one marketed by E. T. Tackle. This will ensure there is no damage to the fish from a gravel bank or twigs. Use a good pair of forceps or a disgorger to release the hook swiftly.

If your quarry is a pike, handling and unhooking is a different game to unhooking a chub or barbel and, just to complicate the

Many good fish are lost at the moment when they are about to be netted due to too small or poorly handled landing-nets. Do not chase the fish. Let it come to the net. Positioning the net downstream will help by letting the fish drop back into it. Fish often spook at the sight of the landing-net or the angler. Clutch control is the answer.

Control the reel with your index finger and be ready to give line if the fish spooks and bolts from the net.

If possible, position the net below the fish so that the mesh is held open by the flow of the current.

Use a landing-net pole of sufficient length to get over the margins.

20in minimum round-pan landing-net

Fig 83   Landing-net in use.

issue, there is a strong risk of deep-hooking if your bite indication is not up to the standards outlined in the methods section.

Confident Handling

If you hook a pike, there is only one way to approach the unhooking and that is with calm confidence, remember you are in charge, not the pike. If you are unsure whether you can cope with handling a big pike, either normally or poorly hooked, then do not go fishing for them or go along with an experienced pike angler and let him show you how it is done. You could even join the Pike Anglers Club of Great Britain!

Forceps

A good pair of long, straight forceps will be invaluable for unhooking both the deeper-hooked pike and those hooked cleanly in the mouth. If the hooks are well down the throat, access is easier through the gill cover with a pair of long forceps.

Unhooking Pike

When unhooking pike, it will depend on the size of the fish just how to proceed. Small to medium-size fish up to ten or twelve pounds can be lifted by the chin for unhooking. This is carried out by inserting your fingers under the gill cover (*see* Fig 84), and sliding them along

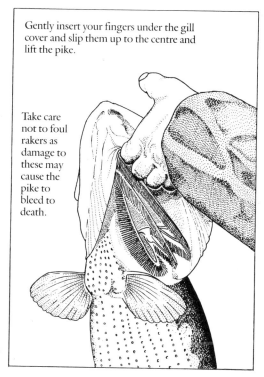

Gently insert your fingers under the gill cover and slip them up to the centre and lift the pike.

Take care not to foul rakers as damage to these may cause the pike to bleed to death.

Fig 84   Chin-lifting a pike.

the edge of the gill cover until you reach the centre joint under the jaw. Take care not to damage the gill rakers at this point. With the hand firmly located you can now raise the fish from the ground. If gently persuaded, the mouth will open and stay that way for the unhooking.

Deep Hook Removal

If your fish is in excess of ten pounds or is a particularly active fish, you can lay it out on your handling mat and place yourself astride it, repeating the procedure of sliding your fingers into the gill cover. This time raise the pike's head carefully and again gently persuade its mouth to open. If the hooks are deep, you can now gain access to them by putting your long

forceps through between the gill rakers, taking extreme care not to damage them. You or your friend should take a firm hold of the trace swivel and pull it tight, release the hook and, if necessary, keep pulling tight. Release the second hook when it is visible. If you approach it confidently, it really is quite simple!

PHOTOGRAPHING

After the capture of any fish, particularly if it is a quality fish, you will have to decide whether you want to weigh, photograph and return it or retain it for a while.

Keepnets

If you decide to do the latter, then you must retain your fish in a way that will not injure or cause any distress. Roach and dace will not come to harm in a keepnet, providing it is large enough (at least eighteen inches in diameter and twelve feet long), and of micro mesh material. Chub and barbel can cope with a short period in a keepnet in an extreme situation. If you intend using a keepnet, then make sure that you use one of the type described and stake it out in a position so that the fish can face the flow. This will mean that it points downstream in a slack margin swim, and possibly upstream in faster flows, with a bank stick holding it in place. Long fish like barbel may not be able to turn around within the confines of a keepnet and great discomfort will be experienced if the water is flowing into their gills from behind.

Keeptubes

With chub, barbel, pike and bream the retaining of the bigger specimens in a keepnet may cause discomfort and it would be wise to retain them, if you really must, in one of the larger

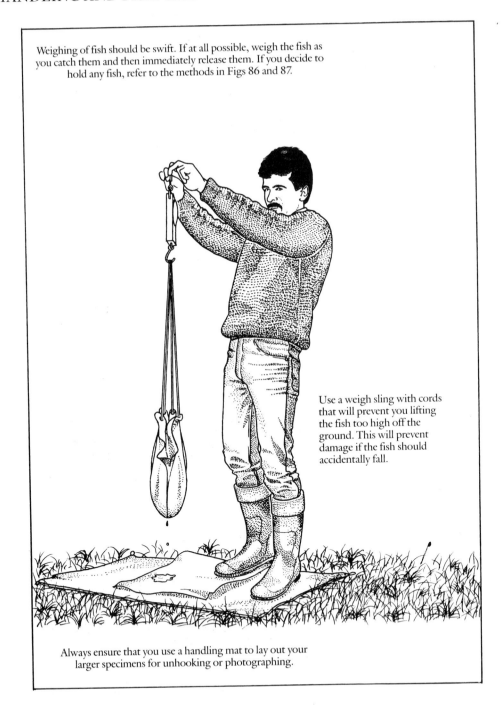

Weighing of fish should be swift. If at all possible, weigh the fish as you catch them and then immediately release them. If you decide to hold any fish, refer to the methods in Figs 86 and 87.

Use a weigh sling with cords that will prevent you lifting the fish too high off the ground. This will prevent damage if the fish should accidentally fall.

Always ensure that you use a handling mat to lay out your larger specimens for unhooking or photographing.

Fig 85   Weighing a fish.

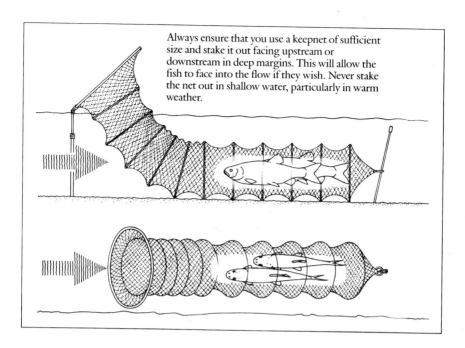

Always ensure that you use a keepnet of sufficient size and stake it out facing upstream or downstream in deep margins. This will allow the fish to face into the flow if they wish. Never stake the net out in shallow water, particularly in warm weather.

Fig 86   Keepnet in use.

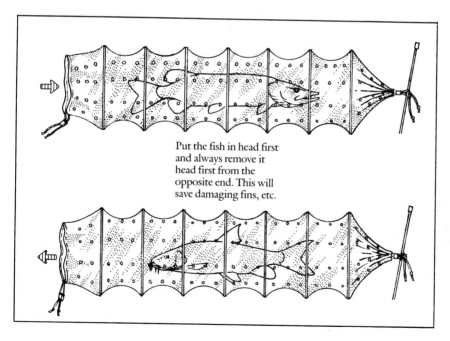

Put the fish in head first and always remove it head first from the opposite end. This will save damaging fins, etc.

Fig 87   Keeptube in use.

Unhooking aided by good forceps.

carp sacks or in one of the new pike or barbel tubes. These are tubes of carp sack nylon material covering a set of hoops similar to a keepnet. They afford fish the comfort of a keepnet but avoid the possible damage of split fins or roughening of flanks from rubbing against the mesh. The dark material excludes a lot of light, keeping the fish passive. The nylon material is full of punched holes which allows the water to flow freely through the tube. Probably the biggest advantage is noticed when you come to release your fish, as you simply untie the opposite end to which you put the fish in. This saves all the effort and discomfort of getting the fish out backwards. As with keepnets the tube should be positioned with the flow, not across it, with fish facing into the flow.

Retaining Fish

One of the main reasons for retaining your fish is likely to be to accumulate a large catch of dace or roach, or one or two large specimens of each species, for a photograph. Whilst this is a natural action you should consider whether it is to the advantage of the fish, particularly with big fish in shallow water during the summer or in a river in flood conditions. If you are in any doubt, return the fish immediately!

Photographs are the main goal when big fish are retained and some thought should be given as to how you go about it, to prevent both disappointment on your part and discomfort for your prize fish.

Photograph Planning

You should plan carefully where the shot will be taken. A pleasant backdrop of reeds, a bush or some other bank side feature will enhance the shot. Wherever you decide on, make sure that there is plenty of soft grass or matting around on which to lay the fish. Whilst you are looking and planning, make sure your catch is comfortable in the water. If you are planning to photograph fish as you catch them and then return them, it may be adequate to leave them in your landing net, whilst you or your friend set up the camera. The important thing is that whatever you do, you must make sure that you have everything ready and in position *before* you take the fish out of the water.

Some really good photographs can be taken at the water side and some of these can be of you actually releasing your fish.

RETURNING FISH

When you release your fish, particularly a barbel which may have fought very hard, you should spend time supporting the fish to make sure it is fully recovered and able to swim. Imagine what would happen to a tired, exhausted fish, shoved back into a river's current. It could be in desperate trouble.

THE FUTURE

If you go to hook and land your fish prepared with good tackle and terminal tackle, and you then handle and return it with respect, there is no reason why you, or anybody else, should not catch them again, as many anglers before you will have done.

We all love to catch fish that have never been caught before and whilst there is always the chance of finding a few, you should take care of them. Many of the fish we catch get caught regularly due to the amount of anglers who fish today. Several of those fish were caught for the first time by anglers who sought uncaught fish and who returned them unharmed. It would be nice to think we will *all* do the same.

Useful Addresses

National Association of Specialist Anglers (NASA)
Membership Secretary
Kathy Fickling
'Kilgarth'
27 Lodge Lane
Upton
Gainsborough
Lincolnshire

National Record Fish Commmittee (NRFC)
Chairman
Phil Smith
155 Hunts Lane
Coventry
Warwickshire
CV6 46J
Tel: 0203 687780

Pike Anglers Club of Great Britain (PAC)
Secretary
Neville Fickling
'Kilgarth'
27 Lodge Lane
Upton
Gainsborough
Lincolnshire

British (Rod Caught) Record Fish Committee
Peter Tombleson
11 Cowgate
Peterborough
PE1 1LZ
Tel: 0733 54084 (day)
      0733 252428 (evening)

Anglers Cooperative Association
President
Allan Edwards
Midland Bank Chambers
Westgate
Grantham
Lincolnshire
NG31 6LE

Further Reading

Bailey, John, *Roach: The Gentle Giant* (The Crowood Press)

Bailey, John, and Miller, Roger, *Bream: Tales and Tactics* (The Crowood Press)

Bailey, John, and Page, Martyn, *Pike: The Predator Becomes the Prey* (The Crowood Press)

Cacutt, Len, *British Freshwater Fishes* (Croom Helm)

Crouch, Fred, *Understanding Barbel* (Pelham Books)

Fickling, Neville, *Pike Fishing in the '80s* (Beekay)

Gibbinson, Jim, *Modern Specimen Hunting* (Beekay)

Head, Len, *River Fishing* (The Crowood Press)

Maskel, Peter, *The Best of Dick Walker's Coarse Fishing* (David and Charles)

Plummer, David, *Tales of a Coarse Angler* (Oxford Illustrated Press)

Pullen, Graeme, *The Graeme Pullen Guide to Freshwater Fishing Baits* (Oxford Illustrated Press)

Sidley, John, *River Piking* (Boydell Press)

Stone, Peter, *Fishing for Chub* (Beekay)

Walker, Richard, *Stillwater Angling* (Pan)

Wheeler, Alwyne, *Freshwater Fishes of Britain and Europe* (Kingfisher)

Index

INDEX